dancing the
tango
in an
earthquake

REALLIFESTUFFFOR**COUPLES** ON COMPETING DEMANDS
A NavStudy Featuring *The* **MESSAGE**®

Written and compiled by Tim McLaughlin

NAVPRESS®

BRINGING TRUTH TO LIFE

OUR GUARANTEE TO YOU

We believe so strongly in the message of our books that we are making this quality guarantee to you. If for any reason you are disappointed with the content of this book, return the title page to us with your name and address and we will refund to you the list price of the book. To help us serve you better, please briefly describe why you were disappointed. Mail your refund request to: NavPress, P.O. Box 35002, Colorado Springs, CO 80935.

The Navigators is an international Christian organization. Our mission is to advance the gospel of Jesus and His kingdom into the nations through spiritual generations of laborers living and discipling among the lost. We see a vital movement of the gospel, fueled by prevailing prayer, flowing freely through relational networks and out into the nations where workers for the kingdom are next door to everywhere.

NavPress is the publishing ministry of The Navigators. The mission of NavPress is to reach, disciple, and equip people to know Christ and make Him known by publishing life-related materials that are biblically rooted and culturally relevant. Our vision is to stimulate spiritual transformation through every product we publish.

ISBN 1-60006-019-6

Cover design by studiogearbox.com
Cover illustration by Chris Gilbert
Creative Team: Terry Behimer, John Blasé, Darla Hightower, Linda Vixie, Arvid Wallen, Laura Spray

Written and compiled by Tim McLaughlin

Some of the anecdotal illustrations in this book are true to life and are included with the permission of the persons involved. All other illustrations are composites of real situations, and any resemblance to people living or dead is coincidental.

All Scripture quotations in this publication are taken from *THE MESSAGE* (MSG). Copyright © 1993, 1994, 1995, 1996, 2000, 2001, 2002. Used by permission of NavPress Publishing Group.

Printed in the United States of America

1 2 3 4 5 6 / 10 09 08 07 06

FOR A FREE CATALOG OF NAVPRESS BOOKS & BIBLE STUDIES, CALL 1-800-366-7788 (USA) OR 1-800-839-4769 (CANADA)

contents

about the
REALLIFESTUFFFORCOUPLES
series

Let your love dictate how you deal with me;
  teach me from your textbook on life.
I'm your servant—help me understand what that means,
  the inner meaning of your instructions. . . .
Break open your words, let the light shine out,
  let ordinary people see the meaning.

—PSALM 119:124-125,130

We're all yearning for understanding, for truth, wisdom, hope. Whether we quietly simmer in uncertainty or boil over into blatant unbelief, we long for a better life—a more meaningful existence, a more fulfilling marriage. We want our marriages to matter—to ourselves most of all, and then to our children and the rest of our families and friends. But real-life stuff—the urgency of daily life with all its responsibilities, major and minor catastrophes, conversations, dreams, and all—tends to fog up the image of the marriage we crave. And so we go on with the way things are.

We can pretend that there's really no problem, that everything is actually fine, thank you. We can intensify the same old way we've been living, hoping that more is better. We can flee—emotionally, spiritually, literally.

Whether or not we face it head-on, real life matters. In that fog there are things about ourselves, our spouses, and our marriages that cause distress, discomfort, and dis-ease.

The REAL LIFE STUFF FOR COUPLES series is a safe place for exploring the truth about that fog. It's not your typical Bible study—no fill-in-the-blank questions, no one telling you what things mean or what to do. In fact, you'll probably finish a REAL LIFE STUFF study with more questions than you started with. But through personal reflection and lively conversation in your small group (you know this is the best part of a Bible study, anyway), these books will take you where you need to go—and in the process bring greater hope and meaning to your life.

Each REAL LIFE STUFF FOR COUPLES book gives you the space to ask the hard questions about marriage—yours and others'. A space to find comfort in the chaos. A space to enlarge your understanding of your marriage, your God, and where those two intersect.

And—with the guidance of the Holy Spirit—a space to discover real-life hope for your marriage that brings meaning to the everyday challenge of crafting a life together.

introduction

Marriage: When two people are under the influence of the most
violent, most insane, most delusive, and most transient of passions,
they are required to swear that they will remain in that excited,
abnormal, and exhausting condition continuously
until death do them part.

GEORGE BERNARD SHAW, GETTING MARRIED (1908)

Kiss me—full on the mouth!
Yes! For your love is better than wine,
headier than your aromatic oils.
The syllables of your name murmur like a meadow brook.
No wonder everyone loves to say your name!

Take me away with you! Let's run off together!
An elopement with my King-Lover!
We'll celebrate, we'll sing,
we'll make great music.
Yes! For your love is better than vintage wine.

SONG OF SONGS 1:2-4

I want you to live as free of complications as possible.
When you're unmarried, you're free to concentrate on
simply pleasing the Master. Marriage involves you in all
the nuts and bolts of domestic life and in wanting to please your
spouse, leading to so many more demands on your attention. The
time and energy that married people spend on caring for
and nurturing each other, the unmarried can spend in becoming
whole and holy instruments of God. I'm trying to be helpful
and make it as easy as possible for you, not make things harder.
All I want is for you to be able to develop a way of life
in which you can spend plenty of time together with the
Master without a lot of distractions.

1 Corinthians 7:32-35

The apostolic writer of these thoughts may have preferred you to stay single and thereby more available for the Master's use. However, you opened this book supposedly because you went and got married before God and everyone, and now you're trying to do exactly what the apostle Paul predicted would happen: you and your spouse are wanting to deliberately spend time and energy caring for and nurturing each other. You've found that all the nuts and bolts of domestic life need constant attention and adjustment. Yet the longer you're married, the more, well, just plain life encroaches on your date night, your dinner conversations, your Saturday brunches out, and your pillow talk.

So you feel torn, stretched, in a vise between that entity called your marriage and coping with one distraction after the other; or, more likely, several at once. For there are distractions; then there are distractions. There are distractions that you can and ought to avoid; then there are distractions that are just part of being married, that you cannot avoid, *shouldn't* avoid, that you just have to muddle through the best you can. These distractions—scarcity of money or time or sex or whatever you wish you had more of, marital roles so fluid these days that you almost have to reinvent what works in your own marriage, the inevitable crises of illness or traumas or deaths, personal treks you must take deep into yourself, by yourself—these are all either good things or inevitable things. Yet in a marriage these good and inevitable things get in the way of being singlemindedly married. This fact is neither good nor bad—it just is.

This is where sincere, albeit simplistic, remedies don't touch such dilemmas. *Just abide in Christ . . . just walk in the Spirit . . . just get into the Word more . . . are you having a regular quiet time?* Your life is way too nuanced for such open-and-shut mandates. Such advice is without doubt worth heeding, but they are remedies that do not necessarily match the malady. And not even maladies, but rather human conditions.

The excerpts and questions in *Dancing the Tango in an Earthquake* are intended not to eliminate the distractions to your marriage (an impossible task, anyway), but to help you see them in a different light, from a different angle, and to help you initiate conversation about these distractions to your marriage among you and other couples—at least between you and your spouse. What you do with the quotes and questions on these pages and the conversation in your living room or around your friend's kitchen table—what you do with it all is up to you. Just a new perspective on a tiresome problem is reward enough for some. For others, action steps are a must (and suggestions are included). Whatever works for you and your spouse and your marriage, and for any others in your small group.

Not all of the excerpts and questions may directly apply to you and your marriage. Maybe you've always been married to the same person and a question about remarriage seems strange. Maybe a career is something you've never seriously pursued nor have a desire to. Maybe you're just married and crises haven't afflicted you yet. That's okay. The encouragement here is to go ahead and take the time to think through the questions. Maybe thinking through them will help you relate to neighbors who are having serious crises of their own. Maybe wrestling with some of these questions will give you insight into sons or daughters and their marriage questions. And maybe, just maybe, stepping into a question you didn't think applied to you may bring long-buried feelings, desires, or issues to the surface. Just remember, this is a safe place to ask the hard questions about marriage—your marriage and others' as well.

how to
use this
discussion guide

This discussion guide is meant to be completed by you and your spouse—*and* in a small group of married couples. So before you dive into this book, schedule a discussion group. Maybe the two of you already belong to a couples group. That works just fine. Or maybe you know three or four couples who could do coffee once a week. That works, too. Ask around. You'll be surprised how many of your coworkers, teammates, or neighbors would be interested in a small-group study—especially a study like this that doesn't require vast biblical knowledge. A group of three or four couples is optimal—any bigger and one or more members will likely be shut out of discussions. Or your small group can be only you two and another couple. Choose a couple who's not afraid to talk with you honestly and authentically about themselves. Make sure all participants have their own copies of this book.

1. *Read* the Bible passages and other readings in each lesson as a couple or on your own. Let it all soak in. Then use the white space provided to "think out loud on paper." Note content in the readings that troubles you, inspires you, confuses you, or challenges you. Be honest. Be bold. Don't shy away from the hard things. If you don't understand the passage, say so to your spouse, to your group. If you don't agree, say that, too. You may choose to cover a lesson in one thirty- to forty-five-minute focused session. Or perhaps you'll spend twenty minutes a day on the readings.

2. *Think* about what you read. Think about what you wrote. Always ask, "What does this mean?" and "Why does this matter?" about the readings. Compare different Bible translations. Respond to the questions we've provided. You may have a lot to say on one topic, little on another. Allow the experience of others to broaden your experience. You'll be stretched here—called upon to evaluate what you've discovered and asked to make practical sense of it. In a group, that stretching can be painful and sometimes embarrassing. But your willingness to be transparent—your openness to the possibility of personal growth—will reap great rewards.

3. *Pray* as you go through the entire session: before you read a word, in the middle of your thinking process, when you get stuck on a concept or passage, and as you approach the time when you'll explore these passages and thoughts together in a small group. Pray with your spouse, pray by yourself. Pray for inspiration, pray in frustration. Speak your prayers, write your prayers in this book, or let your silence be a prayer.

4. *Live.* (That's "live" as in rhymes with "give," as in "Give me something that will benefit my marriage.") Before you and your spouse meet with your small group, complete as much of this section as you can (particularly the "What I Want to Discuss" section at the end of each lesson). Then, in your small group, ask the hard questions about what the lesson means to you. (You know, the questions everyone is thinking but no one is voicing.) Talk with your spouse about relevant, reachable goals. Record your real-world plan in this book. Commit to following through on these plans, and prepare to be held accountable.

5. *Follow up.* Don't let the life application drift away without action. Be accountable to the other couples in your group, and refer to previous "Live" sections often. (In fact, take time at the beginning of each new study to review.) See how you're doing.

6. *Repeat* as necessary.

small-group study tips

After going through each week's study with just your spouse, it's time to sit down with the other couples in your group and go deeper. Here are a few thoughts on how to make the most of your small-group discussion time.

Set ground rules. You don't need many. Here are two.

First, you'll want couples in your group to commitment to the entire eight-week study. A binding legal document with notarized signatures and commitments written in blood probably isn't necessary. Just remember this: Significant personal growth happens when group members spend enough time together to really get to know each other. Hit-and-miss attendance rarely allows this to occur.

Second, agree together that everyone's story is important. Time is a valuable commodity, so if you have an hour to spend together, do your best to give each person ample time to express concerns, pass along insights, and generally feel like a participating member of the group. Small-group discussions are not monologues. However, a one-person-dominated discussion isn't always a bad thing. Not only is your role in a small group to explore and expand your own understanding, it's also to support one another. If someone truly needs more of the floor, give it to her. There will be times when the needs of the one outweigh the needs of the many. Use good judgment and allow a person extra time when needed. Your time may be next week.

Meet regularly. Choose a time and place, and stick to it. No one likes to arrange for a sitter, only to arrive at the study and learn that the meeting was canceled because someone's out of town. Consistency removes stress that could otherwise frustrate discussion and personal growth. It's only eight weeks. You can do this.

Talk openly. If you enter this study with shields up, you're probably not alone. And you're not a "bad person" for hesitating to unpack your life in front of friends or strangers. Maybe you're skeptical about the value of revealing the deepest parts of who you are to others. Maybe you're just not ready to say that much about that aspect of your marriage. Really, you don't have to go to a place where you're not comfortable. If you want to sit and listen, offer a few thoughts, or merely hint at dilemmas in your marriage—go ahead. But don't neglect what brings you to this group of couples—that longing for a better, more satisfying, less tension-filled marriage. Dip your feet in the water of brutally honest conversation and you may choose to dive in. There is healing here.

Stay on task. Refrain from sharing information that falls into the "too much information" category. Don't spill unnecessary stuff—like, say, your wife's penchant for midnight belly dancing or your husband's obsession with Sandra Bullock.

If structure isn't your group's strength, try a few minutes of general comments about the study, then take each "Live" question one at a time and give everyone in the group a chance to respond. That should quickly get you into the meat of matters.

Hold each other accountable. That "Live" section isn't just busywork. If you're ready for positive change in your marriage, take this section seriously. Not only should you be thorough as you summarize your discoveries, practical as you compose your goals, and realistic as you determine the plan for accountability, you must also hold the other couples in the group accountable for doing these things. Be lovingly, brutally honest as you examine each other's "Live" section. Don't hold back—this is where the rubber meets the road. A lack of openness here may send other couples in your group skidding off that road.

competing relationships

Aging parents, children, a friend who is easier
to be with than your spouse, exes, in-laws

the beginning place

It all began with Just You Two. In adolescence or adulthood you met,
paired off, and usually sooner rather than later you married each other.
The wedding as well as the dating were essentially a celebration of Just
You Two. So was the honeymoon.

Then you came home to jobs and in-town relatives and, often not
long after that, children. And the crisply defined Just You Two gradually dissolved in a puddle of everyday stuff.

For all that your marriage ought to be—your primary relationship
after all—five or ten years into it, you wonder why you spend the least
time with the person you claim to love the most. You spend the most
and the best of your time with your boss or your coworkers or your
clients. If you have children, they're typically next in line for dibs on
your time. If you're a churchgoer, you likely invest time in some kind
of ministry or spiritual practice or committee or small group (like the
one you may be sitting in now).

Meanwhile, your relationship with your spouse—remember, love and cherish, till death do you part, and all that?—gets pushed further and further down the list.

Nor do kids, coworkers, and aging parents have to be consciously cunning to pull you away from a centered marriage. Just plain life does it, even if kids, coworkers, and aging parents are rooting for your marriage. You settle into your marriage, into your home, your community, your church—and the settling becomes a spreading, a thinning out.

The question seems not how to avoid this thinning of a marriage—it is inevitable—but how your marriage adapts, evolves, and rearranges itself to accommodate competing relationships. How do you keep your marriage vital when your wife, having been touched and handled and clung to all day by one or two babies, is on tactile overload by the time you come home and wants no caresses or hugs but adult conversation? How do you keep Relationship Number One crisp when your aging parents are not only living longer than their parents did but want or need regular chauffeuring or care from you? What happens when the household income depends on a close relationship between a spouse and his or her workplace colleague?

So how do you keep your marriage in top form when other relationships compete with it? Perhaps even against it? To what degree can you allow legitimate, even necessary, relationships to compete with your marriage before it begins showing cracks? Use the space below to summarize your beginning place for this lesson. Describe specific relationships in your life, or in the life of your spouse, that you feel compete with your marriage and how successful you've been recognizing and coping with the competition. We'll start here and then go deeper.

read the mother speaks

From *Two-Part Invention: The Story of a Marriage,* by Madeleine L'Engle[1]

Our return to the city and the theatre meant that I had to reexamine many of my ideas about marriage. I wanted to be up at night when Hugh came home from the theatre, to fix his supper, to talk. This was important. But we were no longer free to put our children to bed at two in the morning, to let them sleep until we arose. I got up in the morning with the children and fed them their breakfast and saw them off to school. I do not burn the candle well at both ends. I got overtired and ill. So we called a family conference.

I said to the kids, "Your father needs me more in the evening when he comes home from the theatre than you do in the morning before school. We don't like each other very much in the morning, anyhow. I'll get everything ready for you the night before, but you'll have to get yourselves up and dressed and off to school. When you get home in the afternoon I'm yours, all yours. But if you want a living mother this is how we'll have to manage."

think

- On a scale of 1 to 5 (1 being most traditional and 5 being least traditional), rate L'Engle's marriage as she describes it here.
- Is your marital and family experience similar to or decidedly different from this anecdote? In what ways?
- Do you agree with L'Engle's implied priorities—spouse first, children second? Why or why not?
- Describe a time you inflicted the "If you want a living mother" talk on your children. What were the results?

think (continued)

pray

read   so much for cozy families and faith

Luke 14:25-27; Matthew 10:34-37

One day when large groups of people were walking along with him, Jesus turned and told them, "Anyone who comes to me but refuses to let go of father, mother, spouse, children, brothers, sisters—yes, even one's own self!—can't be my disciple. Anyone who won't shoulder his own cross and follow behind me can't be my disciple. . . .

"Don't think I've come to make life cozy. I've come to cut—make a sharp knife-cut between son and father, daughter and mother, bride and mother-in-law—cut through these cozy domestic arrangements and free you for God. Well-meaning family members can be your worst enemies. If you prefer father or mother over me, you don't deserve me. If you prefer son or daughter over me, you don't deserve me."

think

- Go ahead—you try to figure out what the Son of God meant with these words. (No fair merely conforming your interpretation to what neatly fits into your own theological or marital experience.) Better yet, ask God to speak to you specifically regarding this passage.
- What do you think Jesus would say about relationships that compete with your marriage? Be specific.
- How would you respond to someone who says, "We don't dare dilute our Lord's own words. He said what he meant, and he meant what he said. Which is: Unless you let yourself be cut off from your family and instead let yourself be consumed only with the Lord, you are not his"?

think (continued)

pray

read   office wives

From the *GQ* article "Do You Have an Office Wife?" by Tom Prince[2]

In this office of haves and have-nots, at least I had my first
in a series of office wives, Amy (whose name I changed, like
everyone else's in this piece). For the record, let's stipulate that
the other women in a man's life are great. His wife is great . . .
everything he ever wanted, more than he ever hoped for, blah,
blah, blah. But if he's going to spend all day and half the night
at the office—his prime postcoffee awake-and-alive hours, the
ones in which he can think and speak and do—what he needs
is a confidante, a fellow corporate soldier to share the smirks,
the laughs, the deep, plaintive groans of incredulity, and the rare
moments of self-awareness. . . .

Amy was dating a guy with a wine cellar and a roaming eye.
I had a fiancée and a wedding date. No man was good enough
for Amy, including me. But in our own casual, platonic way, we
became a couple: I didn't have to love, honor, or obey—I merely
vowed to hang out with her at fire drills. We ate lunch together,
mocked coworkers together, and shared the few genuine feelings
that didn't get soaked with cynicism and sink to the bottom of
our souls forever. She kept me from sending hotheaded e-mails I
might later regret. "Step away from the keyboard!" she would tell
me. I kept her entertained. For ten, twelve, fourteen hours a day,
Amy was my work wife. I was her day husband. . . .

The people we make fun of are the people we don't want
to become. By telling a work spouse who we aren't, we're telling her who we are. For many men, this qualifies as intimacy.
Admittedly, the intimacy of a work marriage is often based on
stuff that no one else would get. With your work spouse, it's all
inside jokes and finely honed impersonations that can never be
fully appreciated by an outsider. It is the very essence of You
Had to Be There. Although a lot of work-spousal activity happens
in public places—at a conference table, in a meeting—the mental place you go to in those moments is a zone that no one else,

other than you and your work spouse, will ever enter. When someone you both hate does something profoundly annoying or stupid, you look at each other instinctively, move an eyelash or swallow a certain way, and everything is thoroughly grokked and agreed. . . .

After Amy and I stopped working together (that's one nice thing about work marriage—there's no such thing as work divorce), I cut a wide swath through subsequent jobs. I've had only one wife, at home in Connecticut, but in my career, I've been like some Scripture-spouting, woolly-bearded Utahan, with at least a dozen work wives. They've been to my house, met my wife, held my kids. I've met their boyfriends, been to their weddings, babysat for their children. . . .

Whether at work or at home, marriage is a series of secrets and revelations—oddly specific, occasionally insightful. My wife, for instance, does not know that my biggest fear about getting old is that I'll become one of those little antique men driving around in one of those little antique cars with the top down. She has no idea what I think about clove cigarettes, bad toupees, or black-and-white scarves depicting piano keys. But my work wife does. You had to be there. And she was.

think

- What are the benefits of a "work wife" or a "work husband"? The liabilities?
- How close is this idea to your own experience?
- Is your spouse the kind who likes to hear every detail about your workday? If so, do you gratify him with details, or do you hold back now and then for what you believe are wise reasons? Are there some things at your work that you don't want your spouse to know?
- Where do you draw the line between an office friendship and an office friendship that competes with your marriage? What might be some signals that it is competing?

think (continued)

pray

read desperate tentwives

Genesis 29:14-32; 30:1-26

When Jacob had been with him for a month, Laban said, "Just because you're my nephew, you shouldn't work for me for nothing. Tell me what you want to be paid. What's a fair wage?"

Now Laban had two daughters; Leah was the older and Rachel the younger. Leah had nice eyes, but Rachel was stunningly beautiful. And it was Rachel that Jacob loved.

So Jacob answered, "I will work for you seven years for your younger daughter Rachel."

"It is far better," said Laban, "that I give her to you than marry her to some outsider. Yes. Stay here with me."

So Jacob worked seven years for Rachel. But it only seemed like a few days, he loved her so much.

Then Jacob said to Laban, "Give me my wife; I've completed what we agreed I'd do. I'm ready to consummate my marriage." Laban invited everyone around and threw a big feast. At evening, though, he got his daughter Leah and brought her to the marriage bed, and Jacob slept with her. (Laban gave his maid Zilpah to his daughter Leah as her maid.)

Morning came: There was Leah in the marriage bed!

Jacob confronted Laban, "What have you done to me? Didn't I work all this time for the hand of Rachel? Why did you cheat me?"

"We don't do it that way in our country," said Laban. "We don't marry off the younger daughter before the older. Enjoy your week of honeymoon, and then we'll give you the other one also. But it will cost you another seven years of work."

Jacob agreed. When he'd completed the honeymoon week, Laban gave him his daughter Rachel to be his wife. (Laban gave his maid Bilhah to his daughter Rachel as her maid.) Jacob then slept with her. And he loved Rachel more than Leah. He worked for Laban another seven years.

When GOD realized that Leah was unloved, he opened her womb. But Rachel was barren. Leah became pregnant and had a son. She named him Reuben (Look-It's-a-Boy!). "This is a sign," she said, "that God has seen my misery; and a sign that now my husband will love me." . . .

When Rachel realized that she wasn't having any children for Jacob, she became jealous of her sister. She told Jacob, "Give me sons or I'll die!"

Jacob got angry with Rachel and said, "Am I God? Am I the one who refused you babies?"

Rachel said, "Here's my maid Bilhah. Sleep with her. Let her substitute for me so I can have a child through her and build a family." So she gave him her maid Bilhah for a wife and Jacob slept with her. Bilhah became pregnant and gave Jacob a son.

Rachel said, "God took my side and vindicated me. He listened to me and gave me a son." She named him Dan (Vindication). Rachel's maid Bilhah became pregnant again and gave Jacob a second son. Rachel said, "I've been in an all-out fight with my sister—and I've won." So she named him Naphtali (Fight).

When Leah saw that she wasn't having any more children, she gave her maid Zilpah to Jacob for a wife. Zilpah had a son for Jacob. Leah said, "How fortunate!" and she named him Gad (Lucky). When Leah's maid Zilpah had a second son for Jacob, Leah said, "A happy day! The women will congratulate me in my happiness." So she named him Asher (Happy).

One day during the wheat harvest Reuben found some mandrakes in the field and brought them home to his mother Leah. Rachel asked Leah, "Could I please have some of your son's mandrakes?"

Leah said, "Wasn't it enough that you got my husband away from me? And now you also want my son's mandrakes?"

Rachel said, "All right. I'll let him sleep with you tonight in exchange for your son's love-apples."

When Jacob came home that evening from the fields, Leah was there to meet him: "Sleep with me tonight; I've bartered my son's mandrakes for a night with you." So he slept with her that night. God listened to Leah; she became pregnant and gave Jacob a fifth son. She said, "God rewarded me for giving my maid to my husband." She named him Issachar (Bartered). Leah became pregnant yet again and gave Jacob a sixth son, saying, "God has given me a great gift. This time my husband will honor me with gifts—I've given him six sons!" She named him Zebulun (Honor). Last of all she had a daughter and named her Dinah.

And then God remembered Rachel. God listened to her and opened her womb. She became pregnant and had a son. She said, "God has taken away my humiliation." She named him Joseph (Add), praying, "May God add yet another son to me."

After Rachel had had Joseph, Jacob spoke to Laban, "Let me go back home. Give me my wives and children for whom I've served you. You know how hard I've worked for you."

think

- What relationships with your relatives—your side, in-laws, exes, whatever—feel nearly as complicated by jealousies as the tangled relationships among Jacob, his wives, and his concubines?
- Have those familial tangles been combed out yet? Or are you resigned to simply living with the tangles?
- If you're remarried, is your current marriage complicated by an earlier one? (If you have not remarried, do you know someone in this position?) If so, how?

think (continued)

pray

read   god, spouse, kids, others — in that order

From *Loving Your Husband: Building an Intimate Marriage in a Fallen World,* by Cynthia Heald[3]

One major way [the wife of Proverbs 31] maintained her integrity was by living her priorities. As I have studied her life, I have observed that the first half of the verses list her priorities in order. The first comment about her is her excellence or virtue. This is a good indication that her relationship with God was first in her life. Her next priority is her husband. Verses 13-16 speak of her ministry to her children and her home. Verse 17 tells of her taking time for herself, and verses 19-20 describe her ministry to others outside the home.

Understanding our priorities helps us in making right decisions and commitments.

think

- What is the writer's solution for balancing the demands of the various relationships in her life?
- Have you invested a month, a season, or a lifetime living according to this plan? If so, what are your thoughts about such a strategy?
- What does it look like to put God before your spouse, to put your spouse before your children, to put all that before "outsiders"? Be as specific as you can.
- On a scale of 1 to 5, how realistic do you think this strategy is for dealing with competing relationships (1 being hopelessly idealistic and 5 being utterly practical and doable)? Why?

think (continued)

pray

read   from generation to generation

From the *Mothering* article "Good Marriages Make Happy Children," by Harville Hendrix[4]

Most couples who unearth the roots of conflict in their relationship make a surprising discovery: the trail to understanding the sources of the struggle leads to a reservoir of unmet childhood needs. Viewing their marriage through one lens of childhood reveals direct parallels between the way they feel in their marriage and the way they felt as children. The other lens reveals aspect of their parents' marriage that they have unconsciously re-created with their partner. The model of marriage they tried to escape has followed them to their own bedroom where they, like programmed robots, behave with each other as they behaved with their parents.

At some point, enlightened couples ask: Why are we doing this? The answer that finally emerges is that they are trying to work out with their partners the problems that remained unsolved with their parents. Such an awareness often leads to remarkable changes in attitude. Instead of blaming their parents, they see them as wounded children suffering the parenting failures of their mothers and fathers. Couples get to learn experientially what marital and family therapists have been talking about for years: unresolved childhood problems are handed down from generation to generation.

As this awareness settles in, partners look at each other in a different light. They view each other no longer as "intimate enemies," but as fellow pilgrims on a journey toward emotional healing and spiritual wholeness.

think

- Consider the kinds of relationships explained in this excerpt. Describe one that currently competes with your marriage.
- Is it a farfetched or reasonable concept to you that your marriage competes with your parents' marriage? Why?
- On a scale of intimate enemies to fellow pilgrims—where are you and your spouse? Are you satisfied with where you are?
- Describe the time when you first became aware of something about your marriage that was way, way too similar to the marriage of your parents or your spouse's parents.

pray

LIVE

what i want to discuss

What have you discovered this week that you definitely want to discuss with your small group? Write it here. Then begin your small-group discussion with these thoughts.

so what?

Use this space to summarize what you've discovered about the distraction that competing relationships can be to your marriage. Review your "Beginning Place" if you need to remember where you started. How does God's truth impact the next step in your journey?

then what?

What is one practical thing you can do to apply what you've discovered? Describe how you will put this into practice. What steps will you take? Remember to think realistically; an admirable but unreachable goal is as good as no goal. Discuss your goal in your small group to further define it.

how?

Identify how you will be held accountable to the goal you described. Who will be on your support team? What are their responsibilities? How will you measure the success of your plan? Write the details here.

not having enough

Money, respect, time alone, time together, sex—
whatever you're needing more of, but not getting

the beginning place

It can be maddening trying to discern how much is enough. You make more money than your carpool partner. You have fewer vehicles than your best friend. Thanks to the eight-to-five rut, you're home every night with your family, unlike the long-haul truck driver next door. You suspect that you're less in debt than your supervisor, that you get away with just your spouse less often than your pastor and his wife do, and that your coffee-shop barista carries so few demands on her time that, next to her, you feel somewhere between an indentured servant and a social recluse.

Okay, so what's in your kitchen and pantry right now could feed a family in the Sudan or Pakistan for months—yet you still feel on the verge of not making it. At least you're not among the working poor, like some parents you've seen at your child's school—families with two or three or four minimum-wage incomes who depend on public transportation and the local food bank.

The anxiety of slipping to that level, however, keeps you plugging away at your job, putting in extra hours when you can—and it takes a toll on your marriage. You've struggled financially before, and you remember that being a pressure on your marriage. Now, though, it seems you've traded money pressures for time pressures. Money, you've discovered, blunts some of life's unpleasantness, but not all of it.

Or a dearth of children can be a distraction for many couples who long for their own kids. In other marriages it's kids who cause the dearth—a lack of rejuvenating time between husband and wife, a lack of money to keep the kids clothed and schooled, a lack of sex (see "lack of rejuvenating time between husband and wife" above). Of course you don't resent your kids for distracting you and your spouse from your marriage (well, not usually, at least). Your children are gifts from God, and you cope with that distraction as best you can. If they're distractions, they're blessed distractions.

What is the dearth in your marriage, if any? Is a nagging scarcity in your marriage affecting it? Had you anticipated it, or did it take you by surprise? Use the space below to summarize your beginning place for this lesson. Describe an inadequacy or insufficiency that's a distraction within your marriage. We'll start here and then go deeper.

read   got talk?

From *Mars and Venus in Touch: Enhancing the Passion with Great Communication*, by John Gray[1]

Women are under such constant pressure to be loving and sweet that the freedom to be themselves is the greatest gift a man can give them. Even if he doesn't really understand her feelings, the attempt to do so calmly makes her feel powerfully supported. . . .

When a woman shares negative emotions, she is generally in the middle of the process of discovering what she feels to be true. She is not stating an objective fact. . . .

When a woman has a chance to share her feelings freely, she begins to feel more loving. Sometimes she may realize how wrong, incorrect, or unfair her statements sounded, but in most cases she just forgets them as she begins to see things from a more loving perspective. . . .

An overwhelmed woman talks about her feelings the way she shops. She is not expecting you to buy a particular feeling any more than she is necessarily going to buy it herself. She is basically trying on emotional outfits to see if they fit. Just because she takes a lot of time trying on an outfit or testing an emotion doesn't mean it's "her."

think

- How much room do you have in your marriage to be yourself? Or do you even want that?
- Do you think you have enough emotional space in your marriage to share your feelings freely? Why or why not?
- Do the gender patterns in this passage match your experience, or is the husband in your marriage the "talking" one?
- Trace the development of authentic communication in your marriage. Or did you always have it? If not, was there a pivotal moment that spectacularly boosted your communication?

think (continued)

pray

read   money — can you take it or leave it?

Philippians 4:11-14

Actually, I don't have a sense of needing anything personally. I've learned by now to be quite content whatever my circumstances. I'm just as happy with little as with much, with much as with little. I've found the recipe for being happy whether full or hungry, hands full or hands empty. Whatever I have, wherever I am, I can make it through anything in the One who makes me who I am. I don't mean that your help didn't mean a lot to me — it did. It was a beautiful thing that you came alongside me in my troubles.

Ecclesiastes 7:11-12

Wisdom is better when it's paired with money,
Especially if you get both while you're still living.
Double protection: wisdom and wealth!
Plus this bonus: Wisdom energizes its owner.

think

- "Actually, I don't have a sense of needing anything personally," wrote Paul. How close to or distant from your experience is this claim?
- What afterthought does Paul add to his praise of God for helping him through times of scarcity? Compare various Bible translations here.
- How would you rate the balance of wisdom and money in your marriage — 50/50? 30/70? 10/90? Or —?
- Do you sense a difference of emphasis between Solomon the king (the likely writer of Ecclesiates) and Paul the apostle? If so, where might the difference lie?

think (continued)

pray

read   sour sex

From *Secret Longings of the Heart: Overcoming Deep Disappointment and Unfulfilled Expectations*, by Carol Kent[2]

Bill was an excellent breadwinner and always took care of the financial needs of the family, but early in the marriage there was a breakdown in the physical intimacy in their relationship. Every night after dinner they watched television, and Bill, exhausted from a demanding job, fell asleep on the couch soon after the news. Nancy felt rejected on many levels. Caring for small children all day left her starved for intellectual, emotional, and spiritual communication with her husband. When he hurriedly approached her for physical intimacy without first meeting her emotional needs, she was more than disappointed. . . .

When months passed and Bill's behavior didn't change, she felt "used" when he made love to her without first meeting her need for positive communication. His sexual advances stirred a progression of emotions . . . she was churning with desire for emotional, spiritual, and physical closeness with someone who would *hear* and *hold* her.

think

- What emotions does this passage stir in you?
- Is the scarcity in Bill and Nancy's marriage one of communication or sex? Or—?
- How common do you think these marital symptoms are—his exhaustion and falling asleep in front of the TV, her longings and resentments?
- If Bill and Nancy would heed one word of counsel you had for them, what would you tell them?

think (continued)

pray

read   economically emasculated

From *Stiffed: The Betrayal of the American Man*, by Susan Faludi[3]

Julie turned to me. "When Mike gets involved in something, he jumps in with two feet and the focus is on nothing else. At first I thought, He'll get over it. And three years later, he's still at it."

McNulty tried for some levity. "It's my Waco affliction," he said cheerfully. "Waco-itis. It becomes obsessive for a lot of us, a grand obsession." [McNulty believes that a conspiratorial federal government committed atrocities against innocent U.S. citizens at the 1993 siege of the compound housing a small, armed Christian sect called the Branch Davidians in Waco, Texas.]

Julie shot him a dark look, then turned back to me. "Because he's so obsessed with what he's doing, he's ignoring the family he's supposed to be supporting. He's ignoring his responsibilities."

"I'm focused," McNulty protested.

"Well, there's supposed to be another focus—working in the insurance industry, supporting your family."

"Well, that insurance job went away." He chopped at the onion ever more aggressively.

"Well, I also talked to the secretary in his office," Julie said to me, unrelenting. "The one who was doing all his work while he was doing Waco."

"That's not true!" McNulty sputtered.

"We *lost* our house," Julie bored in.

"That was the insurance business!"

"We'd have struggled but not gone under."

"Look at all the guys I know in insurance who went under. . . . All of my friends who were independent agents, all but one, were wiped out. Yeah, we could've staved off the inevitable for a little longer, but I chose to make a transition, and the transition was from insurance to what I feel will be a good career in filmmaking."

Julie, however, was not interested in transitioning to filmmaking. "I like *stability*," she said. "Look, my dad was a

postman. He went to work every day and he got home at three
o'clock every day."

* * *

And so the stories of the underemployed, contracted-out,
and laid-off men of southern California, and their counterparts
in other regions I visited, illuminated more general male losses,
losses that the later "boom" economy would to some extent
conceal, but not cure.

The economic improvement spelled little relief for the men
I had come to know at job clubs, "retraining" agencies, family-
service centers on military bases, and outplacement offices set
up by aerospace companies like McDonnell Douglas. It was little
relief even for those men who finally found jobs. Something
had been broken inside them, and it wasn't going to be made
right by a boom based on inflated stock-market prices and tem-
porary personnel—a boom that yielded great wealth to the
already affluent and deeded to the average man an insecure job,
a rise in status anxiety, and a mound of credit-card debt. . . . A
categorical shift had occurred and it threatened bedrock concepts
of American manhood. A social pact between the nation's men
and its institutions was collapsing, most prominently but not
exclusively within the institutions of work. Masculine ideals of
loyalty, productivity, and service lay in shards. Such codes were
seen as passé and their male subscribers as vaguely pathetic.
Loyalty meant you were too slow or too stupid to skip out on
the company before it skipped out on you. Productivity was
something corporations and their shareholders now measured
not by employee elbow grease but by how many employees
the company laid off. And service meant nothing more than
consumer assistance, exemplified by a telemarketer trapped in a
cubicle, a phone glued to his ear, his have-a-nice-day conversations preformulated and monitored. Such a profound and traumatic transformation affected all men, whether they lost their jobs
or simply feared losing them, whether they drowned or floated

in the treacherous new currents. In the course of my travels, I would meet men amply rewarded by the quicksilver, image-based new economy, men who, nonetheless, felt, as they would say to me time and again, "emasculated" by the very forces that elevated them.

think

- How does the author describe the state of the American post–World War II man?
- What man in your life resembles some of the writer's observations?
- What does the changing job market, as Faludi has described it, do to a man's sense of worth?
- How would you respond to someone who says, "When American men went from growing or making things to servicing accounts, they lost a kind of spiritual backbone—a loss with inevitable results in these men's marriages"?

pray

read   oil crisis

2 Kings 4:1-7

One day the wife of a man from the guild of prophets called out to Elisha, "Your servant my husband is dead. You well know what a good man he was, devoted to God. And now the man to whom he was in debt is on his way to collect by taking my two children as slaves."

Elisha said, "I wonder how I can be of help. Tell me, what do you have in your house?"

"Nothing," she said. "Well, I do have a little oil."

"Here's what you do," said Elisha. "Go up and down the street and borrow jugs and bowls from all your neighbors. And not just a few—all you can get. Then come home and lock the door behind you, you and your sons. Pour oil into each container; when each is full, set it aside."

She did what he said. She locked the door behind her and her sons; as they brought the containers to her, she filled them. When all the jugs and bowls were full, she said to one of her sons, "Another jug, please."

He said, "That's it. There are no more jugs."

Then the oil stopped.

She went and told the story to the man of God. He said, "Go sell the oil and make good on your debts. Live, both you and your sons, on what's left."

think

- What about this miracle, or this miracle's setting, strikes you as mundane?
- Have you ever had an inexplicable experience like this? If so, what kind of scarcity was filled? Describe the occasion.
- Should we count on miracles like this to supply what we lack? Why or why not?

think (continued)

pray

read   in case you think you don't have enough
leisure time together . . .

From *Toward Commitment: A Dialogue About Marriage,* by Diane Rehm and
John B. Rehm[4]

John: Vacations can impose what feels to me like enforced intimacy. I'm expected to spend morning, noon, and night with my
wife, a demand that's not part of our day-to-day relations. I'm
reminded of the old chestnut, "I married you for better or for
worse, but not for lunch." The adjustment is all the more trying because it's so abrupt. Within a few hours of leaving home,
I'm expected to thrive on this unaccustomed familiarity. Without
goodwill and injections of humor, the new regime can make me
feel confined and even trapped. Moreover, there are few oppor-
tunities that will permit me to escape in a way that will not make
Diane feel rejected. . . .

Diane: I want to start by saying that this vacation, here for
three weeks at the farm and working together on this book, may
be the best vacation I can recall. Being together yet going our
separate ways as we've worked, being quiet when we've chosen
to be, it's just been delightful. Unfortunately, that's not the way
vacations have always been in the past. First of all, we've both
had the difficulty of making the transition from work to play. You
and I don't play together easily. It's not easy for either of us to
totally relax, and I think that's part of the problem.

John: I think it was during a vacation at Caneel Bay in the
Virgin Islands that we learned our lesson. There was really nothing to do but swim, sail, eat, and drink in an admittedly lovely
setting. But the lack of intellectual stimulation and activity left us
snarling at each other. In one of my solitary walks, I came upon
the remains of a dead goat. This somehow typified the vacation.

think

- How common do you think this phenomenon is in marriages? Why?
- Rate your marriage on a scale from 1 to 10 (1 being both of you value solitary time way more than together time, and 10 being both of you value together time way more than solitary time).
- Describe your most satisfying vacation together. What do you think made it so?
- What kind of balance have you and your spouse achieved between solitude and togetherness? Or have you yet? Talk about this.

pray

LIVE

what i want to discuss

What have you discovered this week that you definitely want to discuss with your small group? Write it here. Then begin your small-group discussion with these thoughts.

so what?

Use this space to summarize what you've discovered about not having enough of something, and the affect of this dearth on your marriage. Review your "Beginning Place" (at the top of this lesson) if you need to remember where you started. How does God's truth impact the next step in your journey?

then what?

What is one practical thing you can do to apply what you've discovered? Describe how you will put this into practice. What steps will you take? Remember to think realistically; an admirable but unreachable goal is as good as no goal. Discuss your goal in your small group to further define it.

how?

Identify how you will be held accountable to the goal you described. Who will be on your support team? What are their responsibilities? How will you measure the success of your plan? Write the details here.

ambiguous roles

The culture evolves, the economy veers, and your marital roles
will probably shift, too, whether gradually or suddenly

the beginning place

There are countless examples of nonorthodox piety thriving within the
American landscape, though they rarely make the nightly news. When
it comes to the subject of faith, the media continue to be fascinated
with monks and nuns of the strictest orders, children who become so
devout they will not eat in their parents' homes, denominations that
banish gay sons and lesbian daughters.

But . . . now we're stuck with a world-class mess of doubt,
alienation, women in the pulpit, too many questions, too many
choices. Some people find refuge from the contemporary fray in
received authority. I relish my freedom to wrestle with my faith,
respectful of the sustaining traditions of the past and grateful for
the insights and wisdom of the present. I agree that nothing is
simple anymore. And for that, I thank God.

ANITA DIAMANT[1]

Near the top of the list of unsimple things these days is marriage. And one of the more complicated things about it is nailing down roles—who ought to do what, who ought to *be* what. In Western industrialized cultures these were not questions until the previous century; in fact, in much of the world roles are still fairly well defined: wives work the fields and husbands hunt. Or wives tend home and hearth while husbands labor for wages. Midwifery is fused with mysticism in many cultures, and village shamans are male. In such cultures, or corners of cultures, this is the Way Things Are Done.

In most of Western society, however, marital roles—like most everything else—is in flux. The Industrial Revolution attracted workers from farms to city factories and shops. Cities were (and are) melting pots of races, religions, mores, and lifestyles, and even if you didn't abandon your own ethos, you lived next to a Puerto Rican, shopped at a Chinese-owned store, stood on the crowded train closer to female strangers than you would your own aunt, and jostled Presbyterian bankers, blue-collar unionists, and Pentecostal blacks.

Women's rights, workers' rights—these early-twentieth-century movements helped dissolve the strictly defined roles within marriage. They also acknowledged the illicit side of what is often called "traditional marriage"—affairs with mistresses, trysts with prostitutes, alcoholic husbands and fathers who deserted their families because of shame or indolence or that perennial American urge to start over somewhere else, with someone else.

Marital roles couldn't help but adapt to the changing society. Wars took men to the front and women to the factories. As early as the 1920s and '30s, movies exported lives of Hollywood's rich and famous throughout the country and the world. Marriage lost some of its sheen with the availability and social approval of other kinds of romantic liaisons.

Fast-forward a half century or so. Now men and women hold not just one or two jobs during their working lives before they retire with a full pension, but five and more jobs—and the only pension they can count on is what they've saved themselves. So now who keeps house—or townhouse, condo, or duplex? If a wife earns the lion's share of the household income, what does that do to her submissive role in the marriage (as taught by some Christians and contested by others)? Must the same parent who nurses the infants also rear the children? Have we as a culture arrived at some common sense about parenting, or are we only descending the slippery slope of self-centered amorality?

What roles in your marriage did you anticipate? Did you get what you expected? Have marital roles changed for you and your spouse during your marriage? Have your roles been firm or fluid? Do you prefer firm or fluid roles? Why? Use the space below to summarize your beginning place for this lesson. Describe how ambiguous your roles as wife and husband are and to what degree your roles—or lack of clearly defined roles—have affected your marriage. We'll start here and then go deeper.

read   ancient marriages

From *Marriage, a History: From Obedience to Intimacy, or How Love Conquered Marriage*, by Stephanie Coontz[2]

For most of history it was inconceivable that people would choose their mates on the basis of something as fragile and irrational as love and then focus all their sexual, intimate, and altruistic desires on the resulting marriage. In fact, many historians, sociologists, and anthropologists used to think romantic love was a recent Western invention. This is not true. People have always fallen in love, and throughout the ages many couples have loved each other deeply.

But only rarely in history has love been seen as the main reason for getting married. When someone did advocate such a strange belief, it was no laughing matter. Instead, it was considered a serious threat to social order.

In some cultures and times, true love was actually thought to be incompatible with marriage. Plato believed love was a wonderful emotion that led men to behave honorably. But the Greek philosopher was referring not to the love of women, "such as the meaner men feel," but to the love of one man for another.

Other societies considered it good if love developed after marriage or thought love should be factored in along with the more serious considerations involved in choosing a mate. But even when past societies did welcome or encourage married love, they kept it on a short leash. Couples were not to put their feelings for each other above more important commitments, such as their ties to parents, siblings, cousins, neighbors, or God.

In ancient India, falling in love before marriage was seen as a disruptive, almost antisocial act. The Greeks thought lovesickness was a type of insanity, a view that was adopted by medieval commentators in Europe. In the Middle Ages, the French defined love as a "derangement of the mind" that could be cured by sexual intercourse, either with the loved one or with a different partner. This cure assumed, as Oscar Wilde once put it, that the quickest way to conquer yearning and temptation was to yield immediately and move on to more important matters.

In China, excessive love between husband and wife was seen as a threat to the solidarity of the extended family. Parents could force a son to divorce his wife if her behavior or work habits didn't please them, whether or not he loved her. They could also require him to take a concubine if his wife did not produce a son. If a son's romantic attachment to his wife rivaled his parents' claims on the couple's time and labor, the parents might even send her back to her parents. In the Chinese language the term *love* did not traditionally apply to feelings between husband and wife. It was used to describe an illicit, socially disapproved relationship. In the 1920s a group of intellectuals invented a new word for love between spouses because they thought such a radical new idea required its own special label.

In Europe, during the twelfth and thirteenth centuries, adultery became idealized as the highest form of love among the aristocracy. According to the Countess of Champagne, it was impossible for true love to "exert its powers between two people who are married to each other."

In twelfth-century France, Andreas Capellanus, chaplain to Countess Marie of Troyes, wrote a treatise on the principles of courtly love. The first rule was that "marriage is no real excuse for not loving." But he meant loving someone outside the marriage. As late as the eighteenth century the French essayist Montaigne wrote that any man who was in love with his wife was a man so dull that no one else could love him.

Courtly love probably loomed larger in literature than in real life. But for centuries, noblemen and kings fell in love with courtesans rather than the wives they married for political reasons. Queens and noblewomen had to be more discreet than their husbands, but they too looked beyond marriage for love and intimacy.

This sharp distinction between love and marriage was common among the lower and middle classes as well. Many of the songs and stories popular among peasants in medieval Europe mocked married love.

think

- In a nutshell, what were premodern gender roles in and around marriage?
- Marrying for love was sometimes considered a threat to society in ancient times. What about today? Is marriage considered a threat to modern society? What is the basis for your answer?
- Although to marry for property, political, or financial reasons seems a little ghastly to our sensibilities—or at least coldly calculating—do you see any benefits to the now-outdated practice?

pray

read   moses and paul on gender and faith

Numbers 3:2-6,9-16,39

The names of the sons of Aaron: Nadab the firstborn, Abihu,
Eleazar, and Ithamar—anointed priests ordained to serve as
priests. But Nadab and Abihu fell dead in the presence of
GOD when they offered unauthorized sacrifice to him in the
Wilderness of Sinai. They left no sons, and so only Eleazar and
Ithamar served as priests during the lifetime of their father, Aaron.

GOD spoke to Moses. He said, "Bring forward the tribe
of Levi and present them to Aaron so they can help him. . . .
Turn the Levites over to Aaron and his sons; they are the ones
assigned to work full time for him. Appoint Aaron and his sons
to minister as priests; anyone else who tries to elbow his way in
will be put to death."

GOD spoke to Moses: "I have taken the Levites from among
the People of Israel as a stand-in for every Israelite mother's
firstborn son. The Levites belong to me. All the firstborn are
mine—when I killed all the firstborn in Egypt, I consecrated for
my own use every firstborn in Israel, whether human or animal.
They belong to me. I am GOD."

GOD spoke to Moses in the Wilderness of Sinai: "Count the
Levites by their ancestral families and clans. Count every male
a month old and older." Moses counted them just as he was
instructed by the mouth of GOD. . . .

The sum total of Levites counted at GOD's command by
Moses and Aaron, clan by clan, all the males one month and
older, numbered 22,000.

Galatians 3:28

In Christ's family there can be no division into Jew and non-Jew,
slave and free, male and female. Among us you are all equal.
That is, we are all in a common relationship with Jesus Christ.

think

- In terms of roles, what changed between the writing of these two passages?
- What do you think the apostle Paul's words to the Galatians signify for female Christians? For male Christians?
- Could this be an indication that God's operating procedures can change with time, or is there something else at work here?
- On a scale of 1 to 10 (1 being least and 10 being most), how interested do you think God is in the roles of husbands and wives in homes and churches? Why?

pray

read the limits of equality

From *That Hideous Strength*, by C. S. Lewis[3]

"What would you say—what would the people you are talking of—say about a case like [my marriage]?"

"I will tell you if you really want to know," said the Director.

"Please," said Jane reluctantly.

"They would say," he answered, "that you do not fail in obedience through lack of love, but have lost love because you never attempted obedience." . . .

"I thought love meant equality," she said, "and free companionship."

"Ah, equality!" said the Director. "We must talk of that some other time. Yes, we must all be guarded by equal rights from one another's greed, because we are fallen. Just as we must all wear clothes for the same reason. But the naked body should be there underneath the clothes, ripening for the day when we shall need them no longer. Equality is not the deepest thing, you know."

"I always thought that was just what it was. I thought it was in their souls that people were equal."

"You were mistaken," said he gravely. "That is the last place where they are equal. Equality before the law, equality of incomes—that is very well. Equality guards life; it doesn't make it. It is medicine, not food. You might as well try to warm yourself with a blue-book."

"But surely in marriage . . . ?"

"Worse and worse," said the Director. "Courtship knows nothing of it; nor does fruition. What has free companionship to do with that? Those who are enjoying something, or suffering something together, are companions. Those who enjoy or suffer one another, are not. Do you not know how bashful friendship is? Friends—comrades—do not look *at* each other. Friendship would be ashamed . . . "

"I thought," said Jane and stopped.

"I see," said the Director. "It is not your fault. They never warned you. No one has ever told you that obedience—humility—is an erotic necessity. You are putting equality just where it ought not to be. . . .

"You see that obedience and rule are more like a dance than a drill—specially between man and woman where the roles are always changing."

think

- Name one thing in this excerpt that strikes you as particularly insightful, perhaps even profound.
- Name one thing that's foggy and unclear—or one thing that you understand, but disagree with.
- If "equality is not the deepest thing" in a marriage, then what is?
- How would you respond to the statement that obedience and rule in a marriage are more like a dance than a drill? Why?

pray

read   can the one who made the rules change
the rules?

Mark 2:18-28

The disciples of John and the disciples of the Pharisees made a
practice of fasting. Some people confronted Jesus: "Why do the
followers of John and the Pharisees take on the discipline of
fasting, but your followers don't?"

Jesus said, "When you're celebrating a wedding, you don't
skimp on the cake and wine. You feast. Later you may need to
pull in your belt, but not now. As long as the bride and groom
are with you, you have a good time. No one throws cold water
on a friendly bonfire. This is Kingdom Come!"

He went on, "No one cuts up a fine silk scarf to patch old
work clothes; you want fabrics that match. And you don't put
your wine in cracked bottles."

One Sabbath day he was walking through a field of ripe
grain. As his disciples made a path, they pulled off heads of
grain. The Pharisees told on them to Jesus: "Look, your disciples
are breaking Sabbath rules!"

Jesus said, "Really? Haven't you ever read what David did
when he was hungry, along with those who were with him? How
he entered the sanctuary and ate fresh bread off the altar, with
the Chief Priest Abiathar right there watching—holy bread that
no one but priests were allowed to eat—and handed it out to his
companions?" Then Jesus said, "The Sabbath was made to serve
us; we weren't made to serve the Sabbath. The Son of Man is no
lackey to the Sabbath. He's in charge!"

From *Dangerous Wonder: The Adventure of Childlike Faith*, by Mike Yaconelli[4]

Every time the disciples started establishing rules—no children near Jesus; don't let the crowd touch Jesus; don't talk
to Samaritan women; don't let people waste expensive
perfumes—Jesus told them to knock it off, and His rebuke was

usually followed by a lecture that said, "You still don't get it! We are not substituting religious rules with our rules. We are substituting religious rules with *Me!*" Jesus kept saying "Follow *Me*," not "follow My rules." So most of us have spent our Christian lives learning what we can't do instead of celebrating what we can do in Jesus.

What a tragedy. What a misunderstanding of who Jesus is. It was Jesus who taught us how to *break* the rules.

It was Jesus who touched lepers, *against the rules*. (No one was to touch a leper.)

It was Jesus who broke the Sabbath, *against the rules*. (The Pharisees had thousands of rules against working on the Sabbath.)

It was Jesus who forgave people of their sins, *against the rules*. (Adulterers were to be stoned, not forgiven.) . . .

What is it you and I are afraid to abandon? Our comfort? Our schedules? Our careers? Our money? Our possessions? Our security? Our theology? Our need for certainty? Our fear of making a mistake? Our parents' expectations?

think

- What do you think Jesus is advocating with the metaphors about the silk scarf and cracked bottles?
- If Jesus is not a slave to rules but the one in charge—and if he spoke admiringly of King David, who ate the bread off the sanctuary altar (clearly contrary to the Law; see Leviticus 24:5-9)—what could this mean for time-honored rules about roles in marriage?
- Do you believe Jesus was as much of a rule breaker as Yaconelli asserts? Why or why not?
- Where do you draw the line between the Pharisees' Sabbath rules that Jesus overruled and eternal verities that ought never change? How do you come to those conclusions?

think (continued)

pray

read   who deals with domesticity's dirt?

From *The Truth Behind the Mommy Wars: Who Decides What Makes a Good Mother?* by Miriam Peskowitz[5]

We need to be able to talk honestly about domestic life in its details. In the apparent triviality of who keeps the grocery list and who swishes away the icky stuff from the bathroom sink rests the major gender and work distinction of Western civilization: Domestic equals private equals women, combined with its putative opposite, work equals public equals men. I'm here to say that if we are to solve our frustrations with family life and mothering and paid work, we must go directly to this elemental distinction and change it, for real this time.

think

- Do you agree or disagree with these words? Why?
- In your marriage, who is ultimately responsible for making sure there's enough food in the house? Has this duty changed hands at all during the course of your marriage?
- Do you think there is scriptural weight behind one way that domestic duties are divided? If so, what way would that be?
- Reflect on how your domestic roles have been or could have been a distraction at times.

think (continued)

pray

read   he's not afraid of questions

From *Dangerous Wonder: The Adventure of Childlike Faith*, by Mike Yaconelli[6]

Curiosity requires courage. You must be willing to ask questions even when they threaten everyone around you. Faith is more than believing; it is an act of courage, a bold grasping of God's truth. Faith is a wrestling match with God, an intense struggle with truth in an attempt to squeeze every bit of knowledge out of it. Curiosity is the shape of our hunger for God. We question God without apology, we march into the presence of God bringing our armfuls of questions—without fear—because God is not afraid of them. People are afraid. Institutions are afraid. But God is not.

think

- If your marriage is unique, the roles you and your spouse carve out for yourselves will probably be unique, too—at least compared to your families of origin and maybe compared to your social circle. If this describes you in even a small way, what kind of courage have you had to summon?
- What questions about your marital roles would you like to march into the presence of God with and get some answers?
- How comfortable are you with the idea of questioning God?
- Where does that comfort or discomfort come from?
- Within the parameters of your marriage, when have you found yourselves at odds with an institution, but at peace with God?

think (continued)

pray

LIVE

what i want to discuss

What have you discovered this week that you definitely want to discuss with your small group? Write it here. Then begin your small-group discussion with these thoughts.

so what?

Use this space to summarize what you've discovered about the roles you and your spouse play in your marriage—especially roles that are ambiguous, nebulous, and changing. Review your "Beginning Place" if you need to remember where you started. How does God's truth impact the next step in your journey?

then what?

What is one practical thing you can do to apply what you've discovered? Describe how you will put this into practice. What steps will you take? Remember to think realistically; an admirable but unreachable goal is as good as no goal. Discuss your goal in your small group to further define it.

how?

Identify how you will be held accountable to the goal you described. Who will be on your support team? What are their responsibilities? How will you measure the success of your plan? Write the details here.

crisis

Death, injury, or severe illness in the family,
an excruciatingly high-maintenance child,
whatever suddenly and traumatically afflicts your marriage

the beginning place

Every marriage has its cracks, and a crisis tends to widen them. A serious accident, an extended illness, death of a child or parent, unemployment. We bring into our marriages, usually unconsciously, all the threads of our experience and expectations, assumptions, and fears. A crisis often shatters those expectations and confirms those fears.

It was an imperial marriage that was distracted by a young prince's hemophilia—the empire itself was distracted, in fact, and eventually the entire world beyond it. Alexei Romanov, you may recall, was the fifth child and only son of Nicholas II and his wife, Alexandra, the last emperor and empress of czarist Russia. The last, thanks to the Bolshevik Revolution of 1917, which murdered the imperial family and replaced them with Lenin's Marxist regime. Yet what so weakened the czar's hold on the government and allowed a revolution to take root?

A family crisis, some historians say. The hemophilia of the young heir to the throne put him in daily danger of bleeding to death by means of the slightest bruise or cut, and the strain of protecting her son only exacerbated Alexandra's mysticism and superstition. The manipulative mystic Rasputin became not only a holy man to her, but also an adviser of sorts, and not only about Alexei's treatment. Common citizens as well as government officials, lamenting the emperor's absence (Nicholas spent much of World War I at the front), suspected Rasputin's influence through Alexandra in state matters. An armed revolution looked downright stable compared to a government headed by a superstitious empress desperate for her son's healing.

Your crisis may not shake the world, like the Romanovs', but it shakes your world and probably your marriage in particular. The infertility of the matriarch Sarai shook her small nomadic world, and the jarring reached her marriage:

> Sarai said to Abram, "GOD has not seen fit to let me have a child. Sleep with my maid. Maybe I can get a family from her." Abram agreed to do what Sarai said.
>
> So Sarai, Abram's wife, took her Egyptian maid Hagar and gave her to her husband Abram as a wife. Abram had been living ten years in Canaan when this took place. He slept with Hagar and she got pregnant. When she learned she was pregnant, she looked down on her mistress.
>
> Sarai told Abram, "It's all your fault that I'm suffering this abuse. I put my maid in bed with you and the minute she knows she's pregnant, she treats me like I'm nothing. May God decide which of us is right."
>
> "You decide," said Abram. "Your maid is your business."
>
> Sarai was abusive to Hagar and she ran away. (Genesis 16:2-6)

But, you point out, Sarai herself precipitated this crisis. Granted—yet many crises are directly or indirectly triggered by *someone*, if not yourself, and the result is the same: pressure on your marriage, a distraction to cultivating a rich, unified life with your wife or husband.

So what crisis are you experiencing—or have you already weathered, or might you anticipate—that is distracting you and your spouse from the business of crafting a strong and delightful marriage? What has the crisis revealed about your marriage? Did the effects on your marriage take you by surprise, or did you anticipate the additional marital stresses? Use the space below to summarize your beginning place for this lesson. Describe how a crisis (not a marital crisis) affected your marriage or the marriage of someone you know well. How did you or your friends respond? We'll start here and then go deeper.

read   total upheaval

From *Amazing Grace: A Vocabulary of Faith,* by Kathleen Norris[1]

[When the author's husband was hospitalized for severe depression—and with no insurance—she stayed near the hospital for several weeks with some Benedictine women.]

During the next few weeks, I held fast to my grandmother Totten's Bible and also the Breviary a monk had given me a few months before. And I learned a great deal about prayer. My daily immersion into praying the psalms was not an escape but gave me perspective on the so-called "real world" of doctors, lawyers, and the insurance company that I had to deal with every day. The psalms became the framework on which to hang so much that I was learning: what a psychiatrist means by "extreme melancholia," for example, seemed close to what I found in Psalm 38. My husband had allowed an unspecified "guilt" to overwhelm him, and "the very light [had] gone from [his] eyes" (v. 10, Grail). With the help of a sympathetic lawyer who gave me a discounted rate, I discovered a catch-22 in medical insurance: when mental illness causes a person to stop paying insurance premiums, Blue Cross can drop you even though the illness is covered in the policy. Being an insurance company, they are only too willing to cancel the policy of anyone who might actually need insurance. Detachment, and the practice of prayer, allowed me to shrug this off and move on, concentrating my energies on the truly important things, like my husband's getting well, and our marriage rising from the ashes.

think

- Has your marriage been undermined by depression—if not that of yourself, then perhaps a spouse or a family member? Talk about this if you can.

- Your spouse's getting well, or your marriage rising from the ashes—when was the last time you were compelled by a crisis to a goal like this?
- The writer had Benedictine sisters to support her in her marriage-threatening crisis. Who or what was your tangible support in a crisis that once threatened the stability of your marriage?
- Norris found extreme comfort in the Psalms. What portions of the Bible have comforted you in past crises?

pray

read   a crisis of messianic proportions

Matthew 1:18-22

The birth of Jesus took place like this. His mother, Mary, was engaged to be married to Joseph. Before they came to the marriage bed, Joseph discovered she was pregnant. (It was by the Holy Spirit, but he didn't know that.) Joseph, chagrined but noble, determined to take care of things quietly so Mary would not be disgraced.

While he was trying to figure a way out, he had a dream. God's angel spoke in the dream: "Joseph, son of David, don't hesitate to get married. Mary's pregnancy is Spirit-conceived. God's Holy Spirit has made her pregnant. She will bring a son to birth, and when she does, you, Joseph, will name him Jesus—'God saves'—because he will save his people from their sins." This would bring the prophet's embryonic sermon to full term:

> Watch for this—a virgin will get pregnant and bear a son;
> They will name him Emmanuel (Hebrew for "God is
> with us").

Then Joseph woke up. He did exactly what God's angel commanded in the dream: He married Mary. But he did not consummate the marriage until she had the baby.

think

- In Luke 1 you can read Mary's immediate reaction to her pregnancy. What was Joseph's?
- The Bible doesn't mention the quality of Joseph and Mary's marriage. Use your imagination and make some guesses as to how this pregnancy affected their marriage. How do you think the community reacted to this pregnancy?
- This wasn't the world's first crisis pregnancy, nor was it the last. How does it compare with out-of-wedlock pregnancies you know of?

think (continued)

pray

read   loss as crisis

From *The Feminine Journey: Understanding the Biblical Stages of a Woman's Life,* by Cynthia Hicks and Robert Hicks[2]

Losses in the form of unexpected changes weave themselves into our life's journey. Some of these are easily negotiated, and some seem to detour us forever. They include: being separated by distance from those we love; the conscious and unconscious losses of unmet expectations and dreams; the loss of romance, employment, and job security; violations of personal safety; broken and troubled relationships; and even loss of our youth. All losses are painful as they force uninvited and threatening change into our lives, thrust us out of our comfort zones, and weigh us down with the insecurities of the unknown. . . .

It is an interesting phenomenon of human nature that losses catch us humans by such surprise. Jesus Himself told us that "in the world you have tribulation" (John 16:33). We are also told by James to "consider it all joy, my brethren, when you encounter various trials" (1:2). In other words, as we journey down the path of life, we will occasionally stumble or fall into difficult situations. The Bible tells us to embrace these trials as we would a long-lost friend who unexpectedly appears at our door.

think

- Which crises in the writer's list have you experienced? What particular personal loss resulted from your crisis?
- Did any of your crises occur while you were married? If so, how was your marriage influenced by the crisis?
- How realistic is it for you to embrace crises "as we would a long-lost friend"? Is this an overstatement, cheerleading, stone-sober advice, or—?

- Assuming that life will regularly send crises down your path, is it possible to take preventive action within your marriage, to strengthen it for such times? What would that preventive action look like? Have you taken such action before?

pray

read   a faithfulness verse

From the *Utne* article "The ABCs of Intimacy: A Toolkit for Getting Closer," by Nina Utne[3]

During a particularly low moment in our marriage, I issued a desperate silent plea for something, anything, that might lift us out of the mire. At that moment, a piece of paper that had been tacked to a bulletin board wafted to the floor. On it was Rudolf Steiner's Faithfulness verse. It isn't about sexual faithfulness, but about the dogged commitment to see what is best and highest in those around us. Eric and I said it out loud together every night for a year (sometime even over the phone when one of us was out of town), and we still say it sometimes. I swear it works a potent alchemy. Here it is:

> Create for yourself a new indomitable perception of faithfulness. What is usually called faithfulness passes so quickly. Let this be your faithfulness: You will experience moments, fleeting moments, with the other person. The human being will appear to you then as if filled, irradiated, with the archetype of his/her spirit. And then there may be, indeed will be, other moments, long periods of time when human beings are darkened. At such time, you will learn to say to yourself, "The spirit makes me strong. I remember the archetype. I saw it once. No illusion, no deception shall rob me of it." Always struggle for the image that you saw. This struggle is faithfulness. Striving thus for faithfulness you shall be close to one another as if endowed with the protective powers of angels.

think

- Recall what once pulled you out of a crisis that was affecting your marriage (even if the crisis was only in your head). Something you read? Something someone said? Something apparently random, or deliberate counseling of some sort? What place does that "something" hold in your life today?
- In times of marital crisis—or a crisis that somehow touches your marriage—do you look backward for hope and to replenish your faithfulness, or ahead? Why?
- It is the struggle itself that is faithfulness, the writer says—not having struggled through to some kind of victory. Do you agree or disagree? Why?

pray

read what family secrets can do

From "Skeletons in the Closet," by Natasha Courtenay-Smith[4]

Bigger secrets are those that have a greater impact on family members—such as affairs, or one person announcing that they are gay. But the secrets that affect an individual member's identity—and which everyone else in the family may know about apart from the person concerned—have the greatest impact of all. "Examples include finding out that your mother had an affair and your father isn't really your father, or finding out you're adopted," says psychotherapist Carol Martin-Sperry.

How a family copes with a revelation depends on their "coping strategy." Families with positive coping strategies are those that can talk calmly together, ask questions and accept that while it may take time for things to go back to normal, they're prepared to work hard at being understanding and supportive until they do. "Families with negative coping strategies can't move past their anger," says Martin-Sperry. "They scream, shout and cry until eventually it becomes impossible to talk properly and their relationships are often damaged for good."

However, even if you've got brilliant coping strategies, it can be very difficult to deal with revelations about a person's identity. "This is because finding out that your parents aren't who you think they are brings in to question everything about you and can cause a total identity crisis," says Martin-Sperry. "It stirs up emotions including shock, denial, anger, sadness and the feeling of being abandoned by your real parents." Even if you manage to accept and deal with these emotions, in the long term it will be impossible not to feel curious about your real parents, which can cause further damage. Resolving these issues can be a very long and hard process.

From two anonymous replies posted on the "Advice" section of Berkeley Parents Network to a member's question about the wisdom and timing of revealing a family secret to children.[5]

We have a similar issue. My husband's biological father is out of the picture, as is pretty much everyone else on his side of the family, except his mother. My husband cut off contact with them when he was in high school due to their emotional and physical abuse. My husband's mother lives in the Bay Area with her husband (my husband's stepfather) and our two children are very close to their Gramma and Grampa.

However, we are at a loss as to what to say to our kids when they start asking questions about my husband's biological father. We do want to be as honest as possible, but at the same time we do not want to invoke any unwarranted fears in our own kids (telling our kids that Daddy doesn't talk to *his* daddy anymore because they had fights and he doesn't love him anymore sounds like a very bad idea). So far we have kept it simple, by telling the kids where my husband's father is located, but we have not gone into specifics yet. Our children are both under six. . . .

One thing that is important to realize is that your husband's baggage is not yours nor your children's. It sounds like your husband is somewhat traumatized by the discovery of his paternity. It also sounds like the whole family is scandalized as well. In our experience, if you make it a big deal, it becomes one.

✳ ✳ ✳

I found out at age eighteen that the father I'd been raised by since birth was not my biological father. Since that time I have come to understand how much suffering keeping this secret caused my parents, and how it negatively affected my relationship with my (nonbiological) dad during my childhood.

While I agree with the posts that emphasize the importance of relationship over biology, I would caution anyone with family secrets that just keeping the secret can in and of itself be damaging in various ways. I seem to have suffered the least—finding out was not the traumatic event you might imagine.

think

- Have you ever become aware—gradually or suddenly—of a family secret? Why was it a secret in the first place?
- What were the circumstances of your becoming aware of it?
- How has that secret, or its revelation, affected your marriage?
- Do you believe the distraction to a marriage a secret can cause can be minimized? Why?

pray

read   nothing, no way, no how

Romans 8:35,37-39

> Do you think anyone is going to be able to drive a wedge
> between us and Christ's love for us? There is no way! Not
> trouble, not hard times, not hatred, not hunger, not homeless-
> ness, not bullying threats, not backstabbing. . . . None of this
> fazes us because Jesus loves us. I'm absolutely convinced that
> nothing—nothing living or dead, angelic or demonic, today or
> tomorrow, high or low, thinkable or unthinkable—absolutely
> *nothing* can get between us and God's love because of the way
> that Jesus our Master has embraced us.

think

- Do Paul's pulpit-pounding words fit any crises you've lived
  through? Talk about this if you can.
- How would you respond to someone who says, "Certainly
  there is no crisis, no problem, no lack, no angel or demon
  that can drive a wedge between you and Christ's love. But
  there is no guarantee that any of these things won't drive a
  wedge between you and your spouse. Your relationship with
  God is secure forever; your marriage, on the other hand, is
  not promised that."
- If not here, where in the Bible have you gone for rock-solid
  encouragement that has gotten you through a marriage-
  affecting crisis? If not the Bible, then where did you find it?

think (continued)

pray

LIVE

what i want to discuss

What have you discovered this week that you definitely want to discuss with your small group? Write it here. Then begin your small-group discussion with these thoughts.

so what?

Use this space to summarize what you've discovered about the distraction that crises are to your marriage. Review your "Beginning Place" if you need to remember where you started. How does God's truth impact the next step in your journey?

then what?

What is one practical thing you can do to apply what you've discovered? Describe how you will put this into practice. What steps will you take? Remember to think realistically; an admirable but unreachable goal is as good as no goal. Discuss your goal in your small group to further define it.

how?

Identify how you will be held accountable to the goal you described. Who will be on your support team? What are their responsibilities? How will you measure the success of your plan? Write the details here.

personal journeys

Detours, left turns, climbing, caving—and you know that,
if only for a season, it must be a solo trek

the beginning place

When we start on this journey, we discover a couple of things
right away. First, the way is largely uncharted, and second, we
are all we've got.

Sue Monk Kidd[1]

It's what we trust in but don't yet see that keeps us going. Do
you suppose a few ruts in the road or rocks in the path are going
to stop us?

2 Corinthians 5:7-8

The ancient Hebrews wandered in the desert for forty years while usually being only an eleven days' trek from the Promised Land. A high
point of Christianity was Jesus' low point—on the Roman cross he was
convinced that his Father had left him in the lurch, left him hanging,
abandoned him. The apostle Paul was usually cheerily confident even

after a beating or a night or a month in jail—yet you get the distinct impression that he was playing it by ear (or by the Spirit, and it's often hard to tell the difference).

The path was uncharted for the Hebrews, the Messiah, and the apostle. They did not always see their next step clearly. They were destined to keep traveling down whatever road they were on, but seldom did they know where that road would lead them.

So we're in good company, journeying into uncharted territory without a clue where it will lead us but impelled by something, or Someone, to keep walking. The only glitch is, such a trek is solitary. You would welcome some company, even if it wasn't necessarily "good," but there's none to be found. "GOD, your God, is striding ahead of you," Moses assured Israel. "He's right there with you. He won't let you down; he won't leave you" (Deuteronomy 31:6). You're not exactly calling the Almighty a liar, but you do wonder sometimes why, for being right there with you, he seems downright absent. Or at least deathly quiet.

The solitariness of a journey into yourself, or into God—if that's where you sense God calling you—means, obviously, that you're on your own. It's not that your spouse is unable to accompany you but that your spouse's presence is unhelpful, even interfering. If it's Godwork or selfwork you're doing—which is often the point of personal journeys—the role of a husband or wife becomes delicate: How do you indirectly comfort and encourage your loved one, cheerleading from a distance, as it were?

So are you or your spouse on a personal journey? If so, what kind of a journey is it? What about it (if anything) suggests to you that it must be a solo journey? What effect is it having on your marriage for one of you to be out trekking—actually, probably trekking deeply into something or someone? How is the trekker coping? How is the spouse coping? Use the space below to summarize your beginning place for this lesson. Describe a personal journey you, your spouse, or a married person you know is taking or has taken. What was the destination or discovery of this journey, or what is the intended destination or discovery? Finally, what was the effect of this deeply personal journey on the nontrekking spouse? On the marriage? We'll start here and then go deeper.

read   a spouse's journey, a couple's anguish

From *The Dance of the Dissident Daughter,* by Sue Monk Kidd[2]

I felt alone and unequipped for upheavals such as this. If I pursued this journey there would be so much to unravel, so much to unlearn.

Later I would read Ursula K. Le Guin's comment: "I am a slow unlearner. But I love my unteachers."

I, too, was a slow unlearner. The problem was I didn't have any unteachers. . . .

I told [my husband] Sandy about my plans one evening as we sat across from each other in the den. I told him my world was unraveling. I asked him to try to understand. . . . I told him I needed time alone to sort through it. That I was going to take several days away.

He squeezed the little hump of flesh between his eyebrows. "Don't," he sighed.

He was talking about more than my going away. He was talking about the whole journey, and we both knew it.

I didn't say anything. He kept rubbing his thumb across his open palm. "I don't understand what you're doing," he said. "This journey you're on . . . I wish . . . " He shook his head. He wished I would cease and desist, that's what he wished. . . .

I was silent a long time. I loved him deeply, but how could I deny this journey? . . . Was it noble to cling to passivities and diminishments, to love ourselves so little we smothered any flame in our own souls? . . .

"I have to do this," I told him softly. "I really have to."

His whole body went limp, reminding me of a glove when a hand has just been withdrawn. There seemed no fight left in him. He got up and walked away.

In a moment of sadness I wondered what would become of us. He didn't understand the extraordinary passion in my heart for this journey. . . . I yearned for his support. . . .

I didn't have guidelines for what I was doing. I didn't really

know if what I was attempting was possible. Was there really
another story to be lived beside the one I was living? If so, no
one had ever told it to me. I imagined there was another way . . .
but what was it?

At times near-panic swept over me. What am I doing, what
am I doing? I would ask. What will become of my marriage? my
religion? . . . Is there another container to hold my spiritual journey? If so, what is it? . . .

It was night. I was sitting in an aisle seat on the plane. A
beam of overhead light, thin and yellow as a pencil, drifted down
to dilute the gathering dark. I turned off the light and tried to
sleep but ended up nursing a sense of loss that seemed heavier
than ever.

I ran down the list. I was losing my marriage (at least the
marriage we'd had in the past). My spiritual life was crumbling
(at least the way it had existed before). My career of inspirational
writing might even follow. I was also losing my identity, the roles
of daughterhood that had sustained me, and along with that,
my way of receiving validation in the world. I was losing the
values from my childhood, my orientation to life. I was on this
plane flying through the darkness, and it was not lost on me that
spiritually I was also flying blind. I had no real idea where I was
headed. . . .

I had no idea where to find light, and really it was too soon.
Descent is not about finding light but about going into the darkness and befriending it. If we remain there long enough, it takes
on its own luminosity. It will reveal everything to us.

think

- Although this excerpt doesn't reveal the outcome of Kidd's journey—in particular, the result of it on her marriage—do you think her journey was even worth the risk of losing her marriage? Why?
- How significant a difference is it to you between losing one's marriage and losing the marriage one had in the past? Give this one a little time.
- Does part of you envy her for the journey she's taking, or does the whole idea leave you cold? If you're envious, what would it take for you to start out on such a journey?
- If you were to take such a journey, what would you set out to find?

pray

read a solo trip

Traditional

> You gotta walk that lonesome valley
> You gotta go all by yourself
> No one else can walk it for you
> You gotta walk all by yourself.

Mark 1:12-13

> At once, this same Spirit pushed Jesus out into the wild. For forty wilderness days and nights he was tested by Satan. Wild animals were his companions, and angels took care of him.

think

- Did Jesus walk his lonesome valley by himself, or did he have help?
- Come to think of it, how many lonesome valleys of various kinds did Jesus walk during his three decades on this earth?
- What was the last wilderness you journeyed through? How long did it take you? What kind of care did you receive (if any), and who gave it to you?
- If you could, would you even want to take your spouse with you on such a trek?

pray

read the trouble never ends

Job 1:8-22; 2:3-10

God said to Satan, "Have you noticed my friend Job? There's no one quite like him—honest and true to his word, totally devoted to God and hating evil."

Satan retorted, "So do you think Job does all that out of the sheer goodness of his heart? Why, no one ever had it so good! You pamper him like a pet, make sure nothing bad ever happens to him or his family or his possessions, bless everything he does—he can't lose!

"But what do you think would happen if you reached down and took away everything that is his? He'd curse you right to your face, that's what."

God replied, "We'll see. Go ahead—do what you want with all that is his. Just don't hurt *him*." Then Satan left the presence of God.

Sometime later, while Job's children were having one of their parties at the home of the oldest son, a messenger came to Job and said, "The oxen were plowing and the donkeys grazing in the field next to us when Sabeans attacked. They stole the animals and killed the field hands. I'm the only one to get out alive and tell you what happened."

While he was still talking, another messenger arrived and said, "Bolts of lightning struck the sheep and the shepherds and fried them—burned them to a crisp. I'm the only one to get out alive and tell you what happened."

While he was still talking, another messenger arrived and said, "Chaldeans coming from three directions raided the camels and massacred the camel drivers. I'm the only one to get out alive and tell you what happened."

While he was still talking, another messenger arrived and said, "Your children were having a party at the home of the oldest brother when a tornado swept in off the desert and struck the house. It collapsed on the young people and they died. I'm the only one to get out alive and tell you what happened."

Job got to his feet, ripped his robe, shaved his head, then fell to the ground and worshiped:

> Naked I came from my mother's womb,
> naked I'll return to the womb of the earth.
> GOD gives, GOD takes.
> God's name be ever blessed.
> Not once through all this did Job sin; not once did he
> blame God. . . .

Then GOD said to Satan, "Have you noticed my friend Job? There's no one quite like him, is there—honest and true to his word, totally devoted to God and hating evil? He still has a firm grip on his integrity! You tried to trick me into destroying him, but it didn't work."

Satan answered, "A human would do anything to save his life. But what do you think would happen if you reached down and took away his health? He'd curse you to your face, that's what."

GOD said, "All right. Go ahead—you can do what you like with him. But mind you, don't kill him."

Satan left GOD and struck Job with terrible sores. Job was ulcers and scabs from head to foot. They itched and oozed so badly that he took a piece of broken pottery to scrape himself, then went and sat on a trash heap, among the ashes.

His wife said, "Still holding on to your precious integrity, are you? Curse God and be done with it!"

He told her, "You're talking like an empty-headed fool. We take the good days from God—why not also the bad days?"

Not once through all this did Job sin. He said nothing against God.

think

- Use your own words to describe the kind of journey Job found himself on.
- Consider the characters in Job's journey. What does each contribute?
- What kind of strain did Job's journey into misery put on his marriage?
- Do you think Job's wife was out of line or simply reacting as a human to extreme tragedy?

pray

read   changing chairs

From *The Feminine Journey: Understanding the Biblical Stages of a Woman's Life,* by Cynthia Hicks and Robert Hicks[3]

For four years I left the world of ministry and got involved in business. I seldom attended church or sought any Christian fellowship. I isolated myself from anything that was not associated with my business. I pulled away from my children and from my husband. I decided I was going to "find myself.". . .

I hoped I would find my value and self-worth in working, accomplishing goals, and making money. Little did I realize that through this process I would emotionally seal myself off from my family and my God. . . .

However, the "finding of myself" took a toll on my family. I had changed the family system; I was different. Gail Sheehy wrote a classic work on women's issues entitled *Passages: Predictable Crises of Adult Life* [Bantam, 1976]. In it she writes, "With each passage (or transition from one stage to another in life) some magic must be given up, some cherished illusion of safety and comfortably familiar sense of self must be cast off to allow for the greater expansion of our own distinctiveness." She goes on to say, "We must be willing to change chairs if we want to grow. There is no right chair. What is right at one stage may be restricting at another or too soft." [31]

My pendulum had swung from being a wife and a mother who was so involved in the lives of her husband and children that she had no identity of her own, to being a working woman who saw herself only as an individual who happened to have three children and a husband. In the last two years I have been reexamining my responsibilities as a woman, wife, mother, and Christian. I'm reminding myself that life is a journey and I've just been moving from chair to chair.

think

- Do you agree with the writer that "there is no right chair"? Why or why not?
- Have you changed chairs in the last year or two? What kinds of chairs were they?
- What toll did your chair-change take on your family? Is anyone else in your family, such as your spouse, changing chairs?

pray

read folly and mercy

From *The Virgin of Bennington,* by Kathleen Norris[4]

I will always regard it as an example of God's great mercy and inexhaustible creativity that so unpromising a creature might begin to turn her life to the good. And not only that: the very things that had gotten me into such irredeemable messes were the instruments of my conversion. It was the illusion of love, for instance, that drew me to New York City. I would not have had the fortitude to move there on my own had I not been energized by the folly of romance. And my philandering professor had done me a good turn by setting up a job interview for me at the Academy of American Poets, where I worked during the winter term of my senior year at Bennington, and where I returned after graduation. The woman I was to work for over the next five years proved to be a mentor who would introduce me to the idea of writing as a genuine vocation, and teach me that it was possible for a writer to, in one of her favorite phrases, "live by her wits." And this, in time, would help me summon the courage to move to my ancestral ground in South Dakota and try my hand at freelancing. These are the sorts of connections and transformations that work their way through any life.

think

- The same things that got her into "irredeemable messes," the writer says, were also responsible for her conversion. What specifics does she list?
- What in your experience is similarly two-sided? What great acts of God in your life seem to have sprung from, or been set up by, goofy decisions you made—if not outright sin?

- Why do you think such a view of human events is rarely acknowledged by many churches, who instead believe, teach, and testify that God's direct hand—not your decisions—is behind everything that happens?
- "Your sin is your strength," someone said. Agree or disagree? Why?

pray

read never-ending journey

From *A Year by the Sea: Thoughts of an Unfinished Woman*, by Joan Anderson[5]

"Look, you've slammed one door, but oh, how you've opened another! People develop in aloneness and are only led to the truth after being disillusioned.". . .

I've come to believe that love happens when you want it to. It is an intention, rather than a serendipitous occurrence. Only when one is open to receive and absorb love can it occur.

"You know, I'm beginning to think that real growing only begins after we've done the adult things we're supposed to do," I say.

"Like what?" he asks.

"Working, raising a family, doing community things—all that stuff keeps you from your real self, the person you've left behind."

"So . . . ?" he asks, waiting for more.

"I don't ever want to be finished. . . ."

think

- In what sense do you suppose the speaker meant that working, raising a family, and doing community things all keep you from your real self?
- To what degree, if at all, have you felt this in yourself?
- To some, their marriage and family are what make them real, not mere prerequisites to self-discovery. Do you agree with them? Why?
- Like the writer, do you want your personal journey to never end? Or would you prefer some closure?

pray

LIVE

what i want to discuss

What have you discovered this week that you definitely want to discuss with your small group? Write it here. Then begin your small-group discussion with these thoughts.

so what?

Use this space to summarize what you've discovered about how one partner's deeply personal inner journey can be a distraction in a marriage, and how to cope with such distractions. Review your "Beginning Place" if you need to remember where you started. How does God's truth impact the next step in your journey?

then what?

What is one practical thing you can do to apply what you've discovered? Describe how you will put this into practice. What steps will you take? Remember to think realistically; an admirable but unreachable goal is as good as no goal. Discuss your goal in your small group to further define it.

how?

Identify how you will be held accountable to the goal you described. Who will be on your support team? What are their responsibilities? How will you measure the success of your plan? Write the details here.

passion

Projects, people, principles—
it can be anything you feel intensely about

the beginning place

If it weren't for romantic passions, someone has observed, who in their right mind would willingly leap into marriage—a life of shared *everything*, toilet seats left up (or down), whisker debris left in the bathroom sink, liquids expelled from both ends of a newborn, thousands of hours of sleep lost (when you add hours lost during your child's infancy to hours of sleep lost during said child's adolescence), the prospect of lifelong monogamy no matter what—who in their right mind would knowingly sign on to such a life, if not first blinded to its realities by romantic passion?

"That married couples can live together day after day is a miracle the Vatican has overlooked," quips Bill Cosby. The institution of marriage may depend on its participants entering the institution blind as bats. There'd likely be no entering at all otherwise.

Passion made a couple out of you and your spouse, and lifelong passion is urged you as a couple by well-meaning authors, teachers, and preachers. The only problem is that passions are extreme things, on the hot end of the spectrum, like a fever. You catch a bug, a fever ignites, spikes, and—if it doesn't kill you—subsides.

And so marital passion ebbs and flows, comes and goes, and that's a good thing—at least, that's what we're told. Yet there are other kinds of passions that similarly ebb and flow throughout a marriage. A job search is a kind of passion, if by passion we mean a specific time of super-intensity that, if it doesn't blind you to everything else, at least narrows your field of vision. And one of those aspects of life that is narrowed during such times is your marriage. Or if not a job search, then a budget project at work, a marketing campaign, or overtime that sucks all your energy and attention for weeks or months.

Ministry and church, unfortunately, are common items on a list of passions that distract couples from their marriages. This is a tough one because spiritual passion is a requirement for serious Christian faith, and spiritual passion is demonstrated most measurably in official, recognized, scheduled, and programmed church events. So, many Christians put their all on the altar, dedicate their lives to Jesus, give 110 percent to the spiritual development of themselves and others, look neither to the right nor to the left in their single-minded pursuit of godliness—and, as often as not, leave a neglected marriage and spouse in the wake of their turbocharged ministry.

Some wonder if the hard-charging apostle Paul didn't find himself in this situation. There is strong, though not uncontested, evidence that Saul of Tarsus, aka Paul the apostle, as an up-and-coming Pharisee and likely member or at least novitiate of the Sanhedrin, was at one time married. His letters, however, make it clear that he was not married at the time he wrote them. Some think it is as likely that his wife left him following his conversion as it is that she died and left Paul a widower at some point before he started writing his canonical letters.

Was Paul's single-minded passion for his Lord among the reasons for the dissolution of this apostolic marriage? Who knows? If this scenario approximates the truth—and no one denies that it's a big if—Paul wasn't the last minister to lose a spouse because of his passion in the service of God. Today's church servants whose spouses leave them never intend to neglect their husbands or wives. Perhaps (in this speculated chain of events) Paul's wife just didn't share her husband's new passion for the resurrected God-man of Nazareth—indeed, as a Jewish wife, she was probably scandalized by it.

Whatever happened or didn't happen, the apostle is clear on one point: He felt he could serve God better single than married. For him, spiritual passion and marriage were mutually distracting.

And you? What passionate involvement with projects or principles or people is distracting you from nurturing your marriage? Or what similar kind of distractions do you see in your spouse's life? Describe an intense interest or involvement of yours that has or is interfering with your marriage. We'll start here and then go deeper.

read passionate perfectionism

From *Becoming a Couple of Promise*, by Kevin Leman[1]

Take this test to determine how much of a perfectionist you are. Check all that apply.

☐ When you see a crooked picture on someone else's wall, you itch to straighten it.

☐ Someone has told you, point blank, that you're too demanding.

☐ You feel driven to correct someone else's mistake, even though it was harmless.

☐ You would rather not do a task at all than not do it right.

☐ You constantly have to control the urge to re-do your children's chores.

☐ When you make a mistake, even a small one, it nags at you all day.

☐ You often give in to the urge to tell others what they should be doing.

☐ If someone termed your work "good enough," that would bother you.

☐ You still feel disappointment when you remember losing an important game, contract, position, and so on, in the past.

☐ You would rather be in charge of a meeting than just be a participant.

think

• If you checked two or fewer of the statements, the author writes, you're probably "only mildly perfectionist." Half of them?—you're moderately perfectionist. Six or more? "You're not only too hard on yourself, but you're probably very hard on everyone around you." So how'd you measure up? How much of a perfectionist are you?

- Is it you or your spouse who tends more toward perfectionism in your household? Would your spouse agree with your answer?
- How (if at all) do you think that a passionate perfectionism can be a distraction to a healthy marriage?
- How do you and your spouse cope with any expectations of perfection floating around your house?

pray

read across a crowded room . . .

From *Iron John: A Book About Men,* by Robert Bly[2]

What does it mean when a man falls in love with a radiant face
across the room? It may mean that he has some soul work to do.
His soul is the issue. Instead of pursuing the woman and trying
to get her alone, away from her husband, he needs to go alone
himself, perhaps to a mountain cabin, for three months, write
poetry, canoe down a river, and dream. That would save some
women a lot of trouble.

I am not saying that falling in love is an illusion each time,
and that romantic love is always to be treated with suspicion and
discounted. The whole matter is delicate.

Hebrews 13:4

Honor marriage, and guard the sacredness of sexual intimacy
between wife and husband. God draws a firm line against casual
and illicit sex.

think

- When was the last time you fell in love with—or became
  infatuated with, or developed a crush on—a radiant face
  across the room? If you can, describe the occasion.
- Do you think Bly has some insight here, or do you have your
  own opinions about what's really going on in those moments?
  How essential do you think it is to describe such feelings to
  your spouse? Why?
- How would you respond to someone who says, "It's not like
  I go out of my way looking for infatuation with others. But
  when I do get smitten, I've found that it can actually feed the
  passion between me and my spouse."
- How have you coped with a marriage-distracting passion or
  infatuation for a person?

think (continued)

pray

read   ministry versus marriage?

Exodus 4:15-20; 18:1-6

[God said,] "I'll be right there with you as you speak and with [your brother Aaron] as he speaks, teaching you step by step. He will speak to the people for you. He'll act as your mouth, but you'll decide what comes out of it. Now take this staff in your hand; you'll use it to do the signs."

Moses went back to Jethro his father-in-law and said, "I need to return to my relatives who are in Egypt. I want to see if they're still alive."

Jethro said, "Go. And peace be with you."

GOD said to Moses in Midian: "Go. Return to Egypt. All the men who wanted to kill you are dead."

So Moses took his wife and sons and put them on a donkey for the return trip to Egypt. He had a firm grip on the staff of God. . . .

[months later]

Jethro, priest of Midian and father-in-law to Moses, heard the report of all that God had done for Moses and Israel his people, the news that God had delivered Israel from Egypt. Jethro, Moses' father-in-law, had taken in Zipporah, Moses' wife who had been sent back home, and her two sons. The name of the one was Gershom (Sojourner) for he had said, "I'm a sojourner in a foreign land"; the name of the other was Eliezer (God's-Help) because "The God of my father is my help and saved me from death by Pharaoh."

Jethro, Moses' father-in-law, brought Moses his sons and his wife there in the wilderness where he was camped at the mountain of God. He had sent a message ahead to Moses: "I, your father-in-law, am coming to you with your wife and two sons."

think

- Trace the presence and absence of Moses' wife Zipporah in all of this. Why might Zipporah and her two children have returned to her father's home?
- From what you know of Moses, how likely do you think it is that his passion for the job God gave him caused him to put his family in the backseat, so to speak?
- Is it ever permissible, perhaps only for a season, to put your family in the backseat? Why?
- Permissible or not, spiritually justified or not, describe the last time you put your family in the backseat.

pray

read   the cost

Luke 14:33

> "Simply put, if you're not willing to take what is dearest to you, whether plans or people, and kiss it good-bye, you can't be my disciple."

think

- Think back to your early Christian journey: What was one of the first "plans or people" dear to you that you jettisoned in order to be Jesus' disciple?
- In your reading of Jesus' words, how important is the word *willing?* That is, is Jesus asking his would-be disciples to lose what's dearest to them or to be *willing* to lose what's dearest to them? Is there a practical difference between these two interpretations?
- Do you personally know anyone who has kissed good-bye someone dear for the sake of being Christ's disciple? Talk about this. What is your opinion of this person?
- Where is the line between a spiritual passion that supersedes your marriage and a spiritual passion that distracts you from your marriage?

pray

read   competing with god

From the *Youthworker* article "Why I Left My Husband"[3]

My husband is a full-time youth director. He is extremely dedicated and spends between 50 and 70 hours a week with young people. I think the reason he is so successful with kids is that he is always available to them, always ready to help when they need him.

That may be why the attendance has more than doubled in the past year. He really knows how to talk their language. This past year he would be out two and three nights a week talking with kids until midnight. He's always taking them to camps and ski trips and overnight camp outs. If he isn't with kids, he's thinking about them and preparing for his next encounter with them.

And if he has any time left after that, he is speaking or attending a conference where he shares with others what God is doing through him. When it comes to youth work, my husband has always been 100 percent.

I guess that's why I left him.

There isn't much left after 100 percent.

Frankly, I just couldn't compete with God. I say that because my husband always had a way of reminding me that this was God's work and he must minister where and when God called him. Young people today desperately needed help, and God had called him to help them. When a young person needed him, he had to respond or he would be letting God and the young person down.

When I did ask my husband to spend some time with the kids or me, it was always tentative. And if I became pushy about it, I was "nagging," "trying to get him out of God's work," "behaving selfishly," or I was revealing a "spiritual problem."

Honestly, I have never wanted anything but God's will for my husband, but I never could get him to consider that maybe his family was part of that will.

It didn't matter how many discussions we had about his schedule—he would always end with "Okay, I'll get out of the ministry, if that's what you want." Of course, I didn't want that, so we would continue as always until another discussion. . . .

His "I love you" became meaningless to me because he didn't act like it. His gifts were evidence to me of his guilt because he didn't spend more time with me. His sexual advances were met with a frigidity that frustrated both of us and deepened the gap between us. . . .

Just once I wish he would have canceled something for us instead of canceling us.

think

- Have you seen this chemistry—or lack of chemistry—in marriages you know, in which one spouse is deeply involved in ministry of some kind? How is this story similar to or different from what you've observed?
- Do you think the narrator is justified in leaving her husband? Why or why not?
- Are church workers more or less susceptible to marital problems because of their passion for ministry? Why?
- What would you say to a young couple, just married, and just beginning full-time Christian ministry?

think (continued)

pray

read madly in love

From *Love Poems from God: Twelve Sacred Voices from the East and West*, by Thomas Aquinas (1225–1274)[4], translated by Daniel Ladinsky

We Are Fields Before Each Other
How is it they live for eons in such harmony—
the billions of stars—

when most men can barely go a minute
without declaring war in their mind against
someone they know.

There are wars where no one marches with a flag,
though that does not keep casualties
from mounting.

Our hearts irrigate this earth.
We are fields before
each other.

How can we live in harmony?
First we need to
know

we are all madly in love
with the same
God.

think

- Read this piece again, preferably aloud—and this time as a love poem between spouses.
- What varieties of passion do you detect in this poem?
- What emotions does this poem stir in you? Do you know why?
- Is it unrealistic to think you can take marriage-distracting passion and channel it to or reinterpret it as a marriage-enhancing passion?

pray

LIVE

what i want to discuss

What have you discovered this week that you definitely want to discuss with your small group? Write it here. Then begin your small-group discussion with these thoughts.

so what?

Use this space to summarize what you've discovered about the distraction that passion—for a project, a principle, a person, for anything—can be to your marriage. Review your "Beginning Place" if you need to remember where you started. How does God's truth impact the next step in your journey?

then what?

What is one practical thing you can do to apply what you've discovered? Describe how you will put this into practice. What steps will you take? Remember to think realistically; an admirable but unreachable goal is as good as no goal. Discuss your goal in your small group to further define it.

how?

Identify how you will be held accountable to the goal you described. Who will be on your support team? What are their responsibilities? How will you measure the success of your plan? Write the details here.

career in motion

Upward mobility, improving your station in life, being all you can be—even for all the right reasons, it still has a price

the beginning place

Few of us, we hope, are coldly using husbands or wives as rungs on the ladder to professional success. At least not deliberately. It's simply that your career matters to you, if not as much as your spouse does, then nearly as much. You may not have chosen this balancing act but nevertheless find it necessary to keep both plates, your career and your marriage, spinning on their sticks.

So let's dispense with the stereotype that your job should never rival your marriage. For even when you don't want it to, it often does—these days, more than ever before, at least on a national scale. And while we're at it, let's also lose the stereotype that paints an ambitious person as some kind of materialistic mini-Trump. You may not be comfortable with the idea of an affluent couple paying an *au pair* or housekeeper good money that could be given to missions if the couple were home more and actually took care of their own children and cleaning. But then 90 percent of the world's Christians wonder what business *you* have going to the movies a few times a year: What you spend on tickets and popcorn for one movie could feed the average family on this planet for a month.

The truth is that establishing yourself in a new job or a new career can distance you from your marriage. Even a new schoolteacher spends a year of late nights prepping for classes that he'll breeze through after teaching them for a couple of years. Or a marriage may be sidetracked when a spouse goes back to school for a degree or license, throwing the income-earning burden solely on the other spouse, if only for a season. The distraction to a marriage that a career in motion presents can take the form of an out-of-town or even out-of-state job. It can be tough to not live at all with a person you vowed to live with till death do you part; but marriages have endured far more taxing circumstances. Still, separation due to career at least distracts if not stops a couple from the business of their marriage.

So what kind of distractions has your marriage suffered due to your responsible and conscientious efforts to advance your career? Even with what you believe are healthy priorities, what cost (if any) has your ambition exacted from your marriage? Use the space below to summarize your beginning place for this lesson. Describe the distraction your or your spouse's career has been, is, or could be to your marriage. We'll start here and then go deeper.

read   occasional cohabitants

From the *Wisconsin State Journal* article "Honey, I'm Home . . . Oh, You Live in Ohio," by Brenda Ingersoll[1]

In 2000, 7.2 million Americans said they were married with spouses not living at home, an 84 percent increase over 1990, according to the U.S. Census Bureau. They were not people who considered themselves "separated," which implies a troubled marriage. . . .

"The advantage is that two people can have a career, but nobody likes it. Everybody hates it," said sociology Professor Naomi Gerstel of the University of Massachusetts in Amherst, who wrote a book, *Commuter Marriages.*

"The change is that women are no longer following their husbands. People expect it will make them more romantic when they do see each other, but it often defeats itself. People really need to make time for themselves together."

Sandra George, executive director of the Wisconsin Newspaper Association, has a rented apartment here and drives "home" to Michigan, where her veterinarian husband lives with their two steers, two cats and a dog. She makes the trip three times a month, and said that she and her husband have lived several states apart for 10 years of their 15-year marriage.

"I spend a lot of time on the road," she ruefully admitted, but said the arrangement works well. When she comes home, "he says it's like spring after winter, and so I adore him," she said. In fact, George sees her time in Michigan as a holiday. "For me, it's like going up to your cabin up north, except mine is in Michigan," she said.

George likes being free to pursue her own career. "You're not confined," she said. "In an economy like this, you do what you have to, and absolutely, you can maintain a relationship. I think you don't take each other for granted."

Not all couples can handle the stress of a commuter marriage, said Dr. Harvey Ruben, clinical professor and director of continuing education at the Yale Medical School psychiatry department.

"They have to be very much in love, tenacious, and very creative to find ways to spend time with each other despite a horrendous schedule."

think

- Do you know anyone who lives only occasionally with his or her spouse due to a job or jobs (not because they are estranged)? How are they doing?
- Do separate residences under such circumstances make sense to you, or do you think that even the idea is repugnant? How would the presence of children (not steers or cats) affect your answer?
- On a scale of 1 to 10, rate the typical couple who live apart most of the time because of jobs (1 being they're self-centered materialists, and 10 being they selflessly grant their spouse the freedom to work at a lucrative or fulfilling job and endure the loneliness.)

pray

read   wealth is nice, and so is work

1 Timothy 6:6-8

A devout life does bring wealth, but it's the rich simplicity of being yourself before God. Since we entered the world penniless and will leave it penniless, if we have bread on the table and shoes on our feet, that's enough.

Proverbs 28:19-20; Ecclesiastes 11:6

Work your garden—you'll end up with plenty of food;
    play and party—you'll end up with an empty plate.
Committed and persistent work pays off;
    get-rich-quick schemes are ripoffs. . . .
Go to work in the morning
    and stick to it until evening without watching the clock.
You never know from moment to moment
    how your work will turn out in the end.

think

- If these verses were all the Bible said about work and money, would you say the Bible comes down on the side of "money is good" or "money is dangerous"?
- Thank goodness that this isn't all the Bible says. What else do you recall the Bible saying about money?
- It is in passages like these that some theologians see what they call the sanctity of work. What would make wage-earning labor holy? What could make it unholy?

pray

read two working spouses equals no time

From the *American Demographics* article "Two Careers, One Marriage," by Nancy Ten Kate[2]

> Lack of time is the biggest challenge for working couples, cited by 56 percent. The second biggest challenge is balancing personal and professional life, cited by 39 percent. A male director of business planning with one child says it in a nut-shell: "I have absolutely no time for myself or my friends; not enough time for us as a couple, and even the extended family says they don't see us enough. We both put a lot of time into our careers."

think

- How close to home—your home—are these statistics?
- The affluent can increase or decrease their workload, depending on how much money they want to earn month to month or year to year. Most of us, however, lack this versatility—we pay our rent or mortgage, utilities, car payments, and grocery bills month to month, if not week to week. And because jobs pay as little as possible, most workers don't have the time to work much more and don't have the savings to work less. So, can you blame a couple who decides, for a few years, to throw themselves into their jobs, letting their marriage idle until they can focus on it again? Talk about this.
- Could a job be worth not seeing much of your family or friends for a year? Explain your answer.

pray

read You May Not See Her Much, but When You Do . . .

From *How to Be Your Wife's Best Friend: 365 Ways to Express Your Love,* by Dan Bolin and John Trent[3]

- Set up a "First Monday" lunch date where you start off the month by sharing a midday meal together.
- Leave a message on her voice mail telling her you love her and what you appreciate about her.
- Call every night you are on the road.
- To keep a business trip from being a parenthesis in your relationship, share with her the key meeting or tasks you'll be facing—and even the times of your meetings—as a way of making her feel connected.
- Call her on the phone and ask her out on a date.
- Meet her with a rose when she gets off an airplane.
- Take her with you on a business trip.
- Take time to share upcoming events with her, instead of letting her find out about your schedule when you're talking with others.

think

- Which of these marital tips fit you, your spouse, and your busy schedules best?
- Which of these tips leave you cold? Which ones leave you cold but would impress your spouse?
- Describe the last time a gimmicky idea made your spouse feel like a million bucks.

think (continued)

pray

read   the cat was away

2 Samuel 11:1-11

When that time of year came around again, the anniversary of the Ammonite aggression, David dispatched Joab and his fighting men of Israel in full force to destroy the Ammonites for good. They laid siege to Rabbah, but David stayed in Jerusalem.

One late afternoon, David got up from taking his nap and was strolling on the roof of the palace. From his vantage point on the roof he saw a woman bathing. The woman was stunningly beautiful. David sent to ask about her, and was told, "Isn't this Bathsheba, daughter of Eliam and wife of Uriah the Hittite?" David sent his agents to get her. After she arrived, he went to bed with her. (This occurred during the time of "purification" following her period.) Then she returned home. Before long she realized she was pregnant.

Later she sent word to David: "I'm pregnant."

David then got in touch with Joab: "Send Uriah the Hittite to me." Joab sent him.

When he arrived, David asked him for news from the front—how things were going with Joab and the troops and with the fighting. Then he said to Uriah, "Go home. Have a refreshing bath and a good night's rest."

After Uriah left the palace, an informant of the king was sent after him. But Uriah didn't go home. He slept that night at the palace entrance, along with the king's servants.

David was told that Uriah had not gone home. He asked Uriah, "Didn't you just come off a hard trip? So why didn't you go home?"

Uriah replied to David, "The Chest [i.e., the ark of the covenant] is out there with the fighting men of Israel and Judah—in tents. My master Joab and his servants are roughing it out in the fields. So, how can I go home and eat and drink and enjoy my wife? On your life, I'll not do it!"

think

- Uriah was a career soldier—and if an ambitious Israeli soldier wanted to be recognized and promoted, his place was in the field, on the front. And because not many armies in human history let wives tag along, households were broken up, if only temporarily. What repercussions did Uriah's tour of duty have?
- Granted, this is a brutal example of distractions that can afflict a home with a career-minded partner or two—but what modern lessons (perhaps not as drastic) can you draw from it?
- Are there some occupational or economic situations in today's world that give you no choice but to shelve your marriage for a time and do your professional duty, hoping you can later massage life back into your relationship?

pray

read   when school is work

From the *Christian Science Monitor* article "Improvising a Back-to-School Life: Adults in Pursuit of Degrees Find Different Ways to Blend Study with Relationships and Jobs," by Lee Lawrence.[4]

Adults returning to school face myriad challenges, from raising money for tuition to finding suitable child care and making time for family. Rather than following a formula, each one who takes the plunge has to tailor an approach that fits his or her priorities. It may be an intensive, full-time study blitz or a long stretch of multitasking. But either way, the experience often means a mix of sacrifices and unexpected rewards.

When she first returned to school, Cucinotta's goals were to continue to earn money and spend meaningful time with her husband, Dean. So she chose a flexible program at a local community college—no lengthy commute, no high tuition. She alternates classroom work with online courses and the occasional self-paced videotaped course. . . .

At this pace, it would take Cucinotta four more years to complete her bachelor's degree. To speed things along, she says she's "revving up to apply to the McBride program" for nontraditional-age students at Bryn Mawr, a nearby women's college. If accepted, she will quit work and depend on grants and loans.

Carving out time for relationships

One student who temporarily relocated to another state for graduate work says her boyfriend makes it a point to read books she is assigned. Others use spouses as sounding boards or, as Cucinotta does, enlist their help in prepping for tests, proofreading papers, and discussing the week's reading. "As a result," Cucinotta says, "I've had different kinds of conversations with Dean. We've discovered a whole new part of each other."

Some students, however, prefer to keep school a separate endeavor. "The constant balancing act is horrible," says Tony Neuron, a systems librarian who lives with his wife and two teenage children in Roanoke, Virginia. Mr. Neuron is earning a master's in library science, but instead of "stealing driblets of time from my family," he finds it easier to remove himself for a month or a week at a time to attend daily eight-hour courses at Syracuse University in New York.

Try to keep the balancing act realistic

As a professor in the Gallatin School of Individualized Study at New York University, Lauren Raiken has advised many a returning student.

His first piece of advice is to have realistic expectations.

"If a person is engaged in many areas of life as a parent and a professional, two courses is the maximum he or she should take," he says.

Professor Raiken has found that returning adults "have usually forgotten the amount of work going to school entails, and what it's like to write a paper."

While most students find ways to balance their various responsibilities, he adds, trying to do too much at once can be dangerous to the quality of learning. "Students find they want to spend more time on campus, at the library or talking with professors and fellow students, but they have to get back to their families or jobs," he says.

think

- Have you or a close friend or relative gone back to school? What was the experience like?
- If it was you, and you were married at the time, how did you keep your marriage nurtured while being heavily involved in midterms and papers?
- Think about the balancing act during that time. What words would you use to describe it?
- How resilient did the other spouse remain?

think (continued)

pray

LIVE

what i want to discuss

What have you discovered this week that you definitely want to discuss with your small group? Write it here. Then begin your small-group discussion with these thoughts.

so what?

Use this space to summarize what you've discovered about the distraction that a career in motion can be to your marriage. Review your "Beginning Place" if you need to remember where you started. How does God's truth impact the next step in your journey?

then what?

What is one practical thing you can do to apply what you've discovered? Describe how you will put this into practice. What steps will you take? Remember to think realistically; an admirable but unreachable goal is as good as no goal. Discuss your goal in your small group to further define it.

how?

Identify how you will be held accountable to the goal you described. Who will be on your support team? What are their responsibilities? How will you measure the success of your plan? Write the details here.

hope in the midst of distractions

Decide where to go from here in your marriage, and how to get there

a time to review

We come to the final lesson in our *Dancing the Tango in an Earthquake* discussion guide. But this is not an ending place. With any luck (and the prayers of people who care for you), you've been discovering some truths about your life—particularly your marriage—and have seen opportunity for change. Positive change. But no matter what has brought you to this final lesson, you know that it's only a pause in your journey.

You may have uncovered behaviors or thoughts that demanded change. Perhaps you've already changed them. Will the changes stick? How will you and your spouse continue to take the momentum from this study into next week, next month, and next year? Use your time in this lesson not only to review what you discovered, but also to determine how you'll stay on track tomorrow.

You'll notice that there's a "Live" section in this lesson matched with each of the previous seven lessons. Use this to note your and your spouse's ongoing plans. Talk about your plans with small-group members. Commit your plans to prayer. And then do what you say you'll do. As you move forward with a renewed sense of purpose, you'll become more confident learning every day how better to live with your mate for better or for worse—and with the confidence will come, gradually, more success at becoming the couple you both want to become.

read   competing relationships

Matthew 10:36

"Well-meaning family members can be your worst enemies."

think

- In what senses is this true?
- How do you balance your Christian faith with this dark truth?

pray

LIVE

How does God's truth influence the next step you'll take with your spouse in your marriage journey?

How will you take that next step?

How will you be held accountable?

read   not having enough

Philippians 4:11

> Actually, I don't have a sense of needing anything personally. I've learned by now to be quite content whatever my circumstances.

think

- How can you and your spouse get to this point?
- In the meantime, list the pressures on your marriage that are due to scarcity so you know where the hurdles are.

pray

LIVE

How does God's truth influence the next step you'll take with your spouse in your marriage journey?

How will you take that next step?

How will you be held accountable?

read   ambiguous roles

Galatians 3:28

> In Christ's family there can be no division into Jew and non-Jew,
> slave and free, male and female. Among us you are all equal.

think

- What marital roles do you and your spouse need to rethink?
- What obstacles are there if the two of you opt for roles less
  traditional than in the past?

pray

LIVE

How does God's truth influence the next step you'll take with your
spouse in your marriage journey?

How will you take that next step?

How will you be held accountable?

read crisis

Romans 8:35

> Do you think anyone is going to be able to drive a wedge
> between us and Christ's love for us? There is no way! Not
> trouble, not hard times . . .

think

- What crisis are you in, or what crisis can you anticipate, that
  you suspect will tax your marriage?
- What steps can you take now to safeguard your marriage?

pray

LIVE

How does God's truth influence the next step you'll take with your
spouse in your marriage journey?

How will you take that next step?

How will you be held accountable?

read   personal journeys

Mark 1:12-13

> At once, this same Spirit pushed Jesus out into the wild. For forty
> wilderness days and nights he was tested by Satan.

think

- What deeply personal journey are you taking or thinking
  about starting?
- How might your journey affect your marriage?

pray

LIVE

How does God's truth influence the next step you'll take with your
spouse in your marriage journey?

How will you take that next step?

How will you be held accountable?

read   passion

Luke 14:33

> "Simply put, if you're not willing to take what is dearest to you, whether plans or people, and kiss it good-bye, you can't be my disciple."

think

- In what sense or to what degree are you willing to lessen your spouse's importance to you in order to be a passionate disciple of Jesus?
- What does your spouse think about this?

pray

LIVE

How does God's truth influence the next step you'll take with your spouse in your marriage journey?

How will you take that next step?

How will you be held accountable?

read   career in motion

Proverbs 28:19-20

> Work your garden—you'll end up with plenty of food;
>> play and party—you'll end up with an empty plate.
> Committed and persistent work pays off.

think

- What is the effect on your marriage of "committed and persistent work"?
- How can you begin to advance in your career *and* nurture your marriage? Or is it more realistic to take turns concentrating on one at a time?

pray

LIVE

How does God's truth influence the next step you'll take with your spouse in your marriage journey?

How will you take that next step?

How will you be held accountable?

notes

lesson 1

1. Madeleine L'Engle, *Two-Part Invention: The Story of a Marriage* (San Francisco: Harper & Row, 1989), 180.
2. Tom Prince, "Do You Have an Office Wife?" *GQ*, March 2005, http://men.style.com/gq/features/full?id=content_403.
3. Cynthia Heald, *Loving Your Husband: Building an Intimate Marriage in a Fallen World* (Colorado Springs, CO: NavPress, 1989), 104.
4. Harville Hendrix, "Good Marriages Make Happy Children," *i*, December 22, 1993, http://www.gobelle.com/p/articles/mi_m0838/is_n69/ai_14658167.

lesson 2

1. John Gray, *Mars and Venus in Touch: Enhancing the Passion with Great Communication* (New York: Hallmark Books/HarperCollins, 2000), 36, 38, 39, 41.
2. Carol Kent, *Secret Longings of the Heart: Overcoming Deep Disappointment and Unfulfilled Expectations* (Colorado Springs, CO: NavPress, 2003), 117.
3. Susan Faludi, *Stiffed: The Betrayal of the American Man* (New York: Morrow, 1999), 431, 43.
4. Diane Rehm and John B. Rehm, *Toward Commitment: A Dialogue About Marriage* (Cambridge, MA: Da Capo Press, 2002), 132–136.

lesson 3

1. Anita Diamant, *Pitching My Tent: On Marriage, Motherhood, Friendship, and Other Leaps of Faith* (New York: Scribner, 2003).
2. "The Radical Idea of Marrying for Love," from *Marriage, a History* by Stephanie Coontz, copyright © 2005 by the S.J. Coontz Company. Used by permission of Viking Penguin, a division of Penguin Group (USA) Inc.
3. C. S. Lewis, *That Hideous Strength* (New York: Macmillan, 1946, 1972), 147-149.
4. Mike Yaconelli, *Dangerous Wonder: The Adventure of Childlike Faith* (Colorado Springs, CO: NavPress, 1998), 53–55.
5. Miriam Peskowitz, *The Truth Behind the Mommy Wars: Who Decides What Makes a Good Mother?* (Emeryville, CA: Seal Press, 2005), 155.
6. Yaconelli, 40.

lesson 4

1. "Detachment," from *Amazing Grace* by Kathleen Norris, copyright © 1998 by Kathleen Norris. Used by permission of Riverhead Books, an imprint of Penguin Group (USA) Inc.

2. Cynthia Hicks and Robert Hicks, *The Feminine Journey: Understanding the Biblical Stages of a Woman's Life* (Colorado Springs, CO: NavPress, 1994), 134, 159–160.
3. Nina Utne, "The ABCs of Intimacy: A Toolkit for Getting Closer," Utne, November/December 2004, 56.
4. Natasha Courtenay-Smith, "Skeletons in the Closet," iVillage.co.uk, http://www.ivillage.co.uk/relationships/famfri/family/articles/0,,163_181668,00.html.
5. Berkeley Parents Network, "Family Secrets," January 2003, http://parents.berkeley.edu/advice/family/familysecrets.html.

lesson 5

1. Sue Monk Kidd, *The Dance of the Dissident Daughter: A Woman's Journey from Christian Tradition to the Sacred Feminine* (San Francisco: HarperSanFrancisco, 1996), 3.
2. Kidd, 33, 90-93.
3. Cynthia Hicks and Robert Hicks, *The Feminine Journey: Understanding the Biblical Stages of a Women's Life* (Colorado Springs, CO: NavPress, 1994), 19–20.
4. Kathleen Norris, *The Virgin of Bennington* (New York: Riverhead Books, 2001), 18–19.
5. Joan Anderson, *A Year by the Sea: Thoughts of an Unfinished Woman* (New York: Doubleday, 1999), 109, 144–145.

lesson 6

1. Kevin Leman, *Becoming a Couple of Promise* (Colorado Springs, CO: NavPress, 1999), 68–69.
2. Robert Bly, *Iron John: A Book About Men* (Reading, MA: Addison-Wesley, 1990), 137.
3. "Why I Left My Husband," *Youthworker*, Winter 1987.
4. Thomas Aquinas, quoted in Daniel Ladinsky, trans., *Love Poems from God: Twelve Sacred Voices from the East and West* (New York: Penguin Compass, 2002).

lesson 7

1. Brenda Ingersoll, "Honey, I'm Home . . . Oh, You Live in Ohio," *Wisconsin State Journal*, December 8, 2002.
2. Nancy Ten Kate, "Two Careers, One Marriage," *American Demographics*, April 1998.
3. Dan Bolin and John Trent, *How to Be Your Wife's Best Friend: 365 Ways to Express Your Love* (Colorado Springs, CO: NavPress, 1995), 232, 250, 253, 290, 179, 148, 122, 56.
4. Lee Lawrence, "Improvising a Back-to-School Life: Adults in Pursuit of Degrees Find Different Ways to Blend Study with Relationships and Jobs," first appeared in *Christian Science Monitor*, March 27, 2001, http://csmonitor.com/cgi-bin/durableRedirect.pl?/durable/2001/03/27/p18s1.htm.